The Heartbeat of an Intentional Community

The Heartbeat of an Intentional Community

A Spiritual Memoir

Rhoda Walter

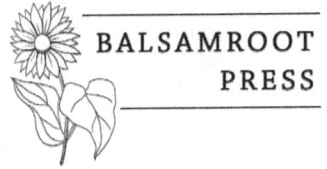
BALSAMROOT
PRESS

Published in the United States by Balsamroot Press, PO Box 246, Winthrop, WA 98862
balsamrootpress@gmail.com

Cover art adapted, with permission, from an image by Deborah Koff-Chapin (touchdraw-
ing.com).
Cover design by Libby Norris.
Editing and layout by Kirkus.
Printer's Ornaments One © Michelle Dixon

The Heartbeat of an Intentional Community: A Spiritual Memoir / Rhoda Walter
ISBN: 979-8-218-24128-5 (paper)
ISBN: 979-8-218-24129-2 (ebook)

Publisher's Cataloging-in-Publication Data provided by Five Rainbows Cataloging Ser-
vices

Names: Walter, Rhoda, author.
Title: The heartbeat of an intentional community : a spiritual memoir / Rhoda Walter.
Description: Winthrop, WA : Balsamroot Press, 2023.
Identifiers: LCCN 2023915312 (print) | ISBN 979-8-218-24128-5 (paperback) | ISBN
979-8-218-24129-2 (ebook)
Subjects: LCSH: Alternative lifestyles. | Collective settlements. | Sustainability. | Spiritual
life. | Autobiography. | BISAC: BIOGRAPHY & AUTOBIOGRAPHY / Personal Memoirs. |
BIOGRAPHY & AUTOBIOGRAPHY / Environmentalists & Naturalists. | HISTORY / Social
History.
Classification: LCC GF78 A3 W35 2023 (print) | LCC GF78 (ebook) | DDC 640--dc23.

This book is dedicated to the nine people who were each essential in creating the collective heartbeat that brought me the twenty most fulfilling years of my life: Monica Wood, Joe Dominguez, Vicki Robin, Evy McDonald, Marilynn Bradley, Marcia Meyer, Paula Hendrick, Diane Marie Ikonen, and Lynn Kidder.

In memory of Joe Dominguez, 1938–1997, and Marcia Meyer, 1939–2018.

Contents

Foreword

We are Helen Gabel and Phil Notermann, partners in life for over fifty years and living in community for most of that time. The New Road Map family was, and still is, a profound influence in our two lives. Their ideas totally changed our approach to several fundamental areas of daily life: finances, living in community, service, death, and grieving. Since you are reading these words, you might be considering hitching a ride on their journey. We believe you will find that it is a journey into what it means to live from one's ideals with as much integrity and authenticity as you can muster.

But the journey you are considering is more than this, as you will discover. Don't let the simplicity and clarity of its words, nor its apparent naivete fool you. There are jewels of wisdom in here and sources of real inspiration about what it means to be human. And, yes, the journey includes the messy, complex and not always pretty ways in which we human beings fall short. It all comes as a package, it seems.

We are living in perilous times. This is apparent to all those who are awake to what's happening in the world today. If there is any promise for a fulfilling and healthy future for our progeny, then surely it will be found in our wild card capacity for creativity and our re-discovery of the fulfillment that can only come through service. This book is about the journey taken by a small handful of baby boomers, ordinary people giving themselves to service. Idealistic, and at the same time practical, together these folks forged a series of discoveries that, surpassing individual creativity, tapped into the immense synergistic power of mutual co-creativity.

We first met the New Road Map folk when we attended one of the last seminars presented in person by Joe Dominguez. (Those workshops became a tape course and later the best-selling book *Your Money or Your Life.*) We were in our mid-thirties working in helping professions (nurse and social worker). The idea of money not being in conflict with our values was intriguing. We immediately started working on the nine-step "FI" (Financial Independence) program. Luckily, we hadn't yet gotten on the middle-class bandwagon of new car/house/kids/travel that most of our generation was boarding. The prospect of more free time now seemed reachable and immensely more valuable to us than more possessions!

Some years later, while we were still employed full-time, but tracking all our expenses and asking those monthly questions about getting true value for the time we spent being employed, Vicki Robin called us out of the blue. She asked if we would like to be interviewed for a TV program about what it was like to be doing the nine steps. We agreed, and after a three-hour recording session in our apartment, we enjoyed our seven and a half seconds of fame on the show *CBS This Morning.*

To our surprise, we learned that Joe and Vicki and crew were actually living in Seattle, as were we. They invited us to dinner, and, as you will read in this book, we entered a field of connection that utterly transformed us. That first very-late-night conversation changed our lives. We never did follow the New Road Map principles as arduously and impeccably as they did, but even "New Road Map lite" added a powerful dimension of meaning and depth to everything we did.

The first thing we took away (beyond the revolution in our financial thinking) was the breakthrough insight that we could enjoy the same deep affinity with other people that we had within our marriage. Casually sharing a big house was familiar from university days,

but living intentionally in community had the potential to offer rich-
ness of connection along with even more power to share resources.
Synchronistically, within a week after that first late-night conversation, friends took us aside to whisper that they would be looking for
new housemates. By the end of the month we had moved into our first
intentional shared-household community. And, thirty years later, we
are *still* living in community, now at Songaia Co-housing in Bothell,
Washington.

Living in community has offered us never-stale opportunities
for growth and joy and connection. We have found support during
illness and companionship during hard times (the pandemic, for
instance). We daily trade smiles and hugs, jokes and chores with
other members. The sense of accomplishment over shared projects
balances the work it takes to keep a large group intact. Of course,
most communities are not as tightly woven as the New Road Map
folk were during the so-called well-oiled machine days. Nonetheless,
community living has held gifts for us in many different iterations.
The author of this book has wisdom and insight to offer, gentle
reader, should you be considering such a move for yourself.

The folks at New Road Map were utterly devoted to changing the
world for the better. While we were working full time, our service-ori-
ented professions seemed quite enough in that department. It took
us eleven years to get to the point where Phil retired completely from
his job leading an addictions-recovery program, and Helen moved to
very part-time clinic and teaching work for pay. It was then that we
discovered the deep joy of service—of being utterly and open-heart-
edly available to the projects and organizations that filled our spirits.

The satisfactions and pitfalls that come from giving oneself to service are articulated beautifully in this little book. Our personal aspirations for bettering the world were on a much smaller scale than
the projects this book describes. Phil engaged in a variety of causes
affiliated with the New Road Map service projects, as well as becoming a leader and organizer in the Dances of Universal Peace. Helen
became a dedicated dancer and got involved in community gardens
and food security. We both currently give many hours supporting our

community and the local peace-dancing group, and highly recommend volunteerism in any form.

By the time Joe died, we were frequent and intimate visitors to the New Road Map household. Joe had held his cancer diagnosis confidentially even from us, but after the last treatment options collapsed, he told us about his impending death. The forthright courage and matter-of-fact attitude he displayed were yet another lesson in challenging the ways our society hides from difficult realities.

The most touching and authentic passages in this book deal with the aftermath of Joe's death and the evolution of the well-oiled machine to a *living system.* Our society is learning on multiple fronts how complex our universe truly is (i.e., systems theory, quantum physics, ecosystem restoration, indigenous spirituality, and so forth). And as climate change and societal disorder accelerate, the need for such systems perspectives grows ever more urgent. *The Heartbeat of an Intentional Community* charts with compassion and honesty the process this ultra-idealistic group of people went through as they made this transition for themselves. We would all do well to follow, as best we can, in their footsteps.

Helen Gabel and Phil Notermann
Songaia Co-housing, Bothell, Washington

Preface

This is the story of my experience living in a small, intentional community for twenty pivotal years of my life. We were a motley assortment of ten idealistic seekers who wanted nothing less than to transform ourselves and change the world. Although we might have been best known for our *New York Times* best-selling book *Your Money or Your Life: 9 Steps to Transforming Your Relationship with Money and Achieving Financial Independence*, our primary focus was always on the question, "How can we be our best selves and better the world through our actions every single day?" But it turned out that while we might have been humans trying to be divine, often we were only too human, and sometimes living in community was hard.

So why did I hang in there when the going got tough?

Our community had a heartbeat, its soul song. Like a hologram—a photograph where any part of the image reflects the whole—each one of us embodied the heartbeat and expressed it, but it was an emergent phenomenon, not something anyone tried to create. It was like a living organism. It was the sum total of how we lived our lives, our collective vibe. The heart began beating in 1970 when four adventurers joined forces to live outside conventional norms, and as each of us came along and resonated with it, the heartbeat became stronger and stronger. Over time, the more we lived from our highest and most noble selves, the more "in tune" we became and the more our resonance created a fuller, richer symphony that was intoxicating to me.

The heartbeat is why I stayed. That steady beat of love, inspiration, intention, and passion. That sense of being cherished for who I was, not who I could be. That continual striving to live my ideals, to fulfill a compelling vision of living in something larger than ordinary reality. I wanted deeply to live that vision more than anything I'd ever wanted in my life. I want to describe for you that heartbeat as I knew and experienced it.

The form our community and our work took was what the times inspired in the 1970s through the 1990s. The 1970s especially were times of consciousness expansion; intense social experimentation; the sexual freedom resulting from, among other things, access to the pill; the New Age movement; and social justice issues such as women's rights, civil rights, and the anti-war movement. By the 1990s, frugality and sustainability had become our focus. Our concern about climate change, resource depletion, and species extinction fueled our work for sustainability. We practiced and promoted frugality, and we demonstrated how to live with a small ecological footprint in a city. We were already grieving the state of the world, and that lent an urgency to our work.

We would have been appalled by the condition the world is in today. All the problems we tried to address are still at play (and much worse), and some of today's most pressing issues did not even appear on our list. While we benefited from the feminist perspective, we were still caught in many of the dynamics of patriarchy. Gender fluidity was barely on our radar. White privilege and the burdens of systemic racism were not at the forefront of our consciousness nor was the concept of climate justice. We were not in the habit of honoring the indigenous peoples of the lands we lived on and visited. (In this book, I do so in the Acknowledgments.)

Even though so much in our world today has evolved and changed since this narrative took place, the story of our community, with its successes and pitfalls, offers a glimpse into another way of living, being, and relating—the heartbeat. It is the story of how one small group of people chose to live and use their energies in service to the world. I hope it will help spiritual seekers and activists alike, young and old, taste an unconventional lifestyle and ways of interacting that are refreshing and perhaps inspire them to create new approaches to being and relating in their own lives and communities.

This book is intended for:

- People yearning to live in community or already living in community. This story could be a valuable resource, shining a light on some of the underlying principles for community living that still hold true while mapping some of the potential pitfalls.
- People wanting to live intentionally or who are on a spiritual search. This book could offer support and inspire you to continue your own journey.
- People interested in how group process can lead to a deeper and more meaningful life.
- Young people. If you are from a younger generation and have rejected the mainstream status quo, this book shows how a group from a previous generation lived an alternative lifestyle. Perhaps it will reinforce choices you've already made or give you the courage to make changes. My hope is that you will find in baby boomers like us solid shoulders to stand on as you reach higher and further than we could, bringing your higher self, your best self, to whatever you are called to do.

Our Community

At our intentional community, known as the New Road Map Foundation, up to ten adults lived and worked together for eighteen years in a rambling house in a quiet Seattle neighborhood. We created and ran an educational and charitable nonprofit foundation, produced a best-selling book on personal finances, and gave away a million dollars to other nonprofit organizations. We also conducted a three-year medical research project on the mind/body connection, staffed completely by volunteers, with the results published in a peer-reviewed medical journal.

We were an unlikely crew. In our early-1990s heyday, there were nine women and one man, ranging in age from thirty-six to fifty-two. We ran the whole gamut of personality types, from introverts to extroverts, analytical to intuitive, bookish to creative, meek to rabble-rousing. Some of us were so introverted that we were more suited to being hermits than living in community. Others thrived on connecting with friends and colleagues, as well as on a wide array of outer stimulation and activity.

Our previous occupations had been: actress, musician, scientist, stock market analyst, editor, housewife, nursing home activities director, computer programmer, waitress, and head of emergency and coronary care units at a major hospital. Our religious backgrounds ranged from Catholic to Protestant to Jewish to atheist. Our spiritual paths had evolved by then to also encompass Buddhism, Sufism, and some self-made paths. None of us were rich, but we each had enough money and possessions to meet our own needs. We were committed to one another, and we tried to live something larger than the usual reality, where we invited one another to live from our highest selves, and it was typical to feel loved, cherished, and accepted for who we were.

The most essential component of our lives together was our individual and collective spiritual foundation. We first came together as spiritual seekers, not to create community or a nonprofit foundation; Spirit was the glue that held us together. While we didn't share a specific spiritual practice or religion, we agreed on basic tenets. These formed the foundation upon which we made decisions, focused our individual spiritual growth, and interacted with one another and the rest of the world. The more we lived these tenets on a daily basis, the more our individual lives functioned well and the more smoothly our community operated.

Our group flourished for many of the years I was part of it, and many of us thought we would live in this community for the rest of our lives. But after one key member died, our cohesion began to wane, and we started bringing to light aspects of our lives together that were not working. When one of us would divulge a long-held dissatisfaction or an ugly part of our shadow (our unconscious group behavior), I would ask, "But surely you see what a beautiful diamond we created, don't you?" Despite many revelations of wounding, hurts, and other shadow material that arose during this time and my own soul-searching over the years, it's this diamond that lives on in me and that I want to describe for you. I won't ignore our human failings, but I want you to be able to figuratively hold this diamond in your hand and see what reflections it might reveal in your own life.

How in the world did we each arrive at this place? What attracted us? Why did we do it—and how? What kept us together? Why, after so many years of living together, did we disentangle and each go our own way? And why were our heart connections not shattered in the process?

This narrative is the interweaving of my personal heart song with the heartbeat of this community—the intertwining of my transformational journey with our collective commitment to love and service. It demonstrates the power of coming together based on a spiritual foundation and with common values and a shared purpose. And it is the story of the challenges that led to the unraveling of our family as we knew it and the ultimately unsuccessful transition from founding and running a non-profit foundation to turning it over to the next generation.

This story is as true of a recounting of the actual events as I could make it, and any errors are mine alone. The ten of us each lived our own stories, and others' experiences, perspectives, or points of view might be quite different from mine. But each person contributed to the heartbeat as I experienced it.

Prologue:
A Doorway Opens

It's September 1983. I am hiking on a trail winding uphill through red, yellow, and beige rock formations in Dinosaur National Monument in northeastern Utah, wondering what I'm going to do with the rest of my life. I've been camping and hiking in the national parks for a year and a half trying to figure this out, and right now, I'm feeling discouraged.

Rounding a bend in the trail, I encounter a short woman with long, wavy, blonde hair, wearing a full leg brace and walking with a distinct limp. She beams at me, clearly enjoying the trail, and says what a nice afternoon it is as she walks slowly down toward the parking lot. I walk on, but the imprint of her happiness lingers, as does my astonishment that someone with her limp is walking this trail, and alone. At this point in my life, I feel as if I'm more disabled than she is. I yearn for that kind of happiness.

Back at my campsite, I've just finished dinner when this same woman walks up to my picnic table and, in the most disarming way, asks me if I'd like to come meet her friends in their motor home. Normally I would be inclined to pass up such an invitation, preferring my lonely solitude over potential awkwardness and having to overcome my shyness. But her happiness and kindness have touched my deep longing, giving me the courage to say, "Yes!"

I don't know it yet, but a new doorway has opened in my life and I'm about to walk through it.

Part I

The Heartbeat Calls

Chapter 1

Opening to the Unknown

I grew up in the 1950s and was a quiet, serious child. I excelled at school, and by high school, my classmates were calling me "the brain." I wasn't so much smart as dedicated to studying hard. My parents instilled in me good Christian values and appreciation of both intellectual pursuits and the natural world. Looking back, I can see that some seeds were planted that would grow and bloom many years later. For example, my sixth-grade teacher had us memorize and recite poems that emphasized character and living one's values, such as "Write me as one that loves his fellow men" from "Abou Ben Adhem" by Leigh Hunt and "I am the master of my fate, / I am the captain of my soul" from "Invictus" by William Ernest Henley.

During the confirmation class I attended prior to joining the Methodist church, I was attracted to Jesus's teachings and wanted to emulate them. But it seemed to me that that would make me even more of a square than I already was with my classmates. Sometime in high school, I read Carl Rogers's *On Becoming a Person: A Therapist's View of Psychotherapy*, and I yearned to be one of those self-actualized people he talked about. But that seemed more than I could hope for in my life. All I knew how to do was live according to my parents' and society's expectations—that is, go to college and maybe graduate school, and then get a job or get married and have kids. I had no idea what I, Rhoda, wanted. I had no idea what introspection entailed and was actually afraid of it.

I attended college in the late 1960s at the height of the counter-cultural movement. Even though I was shy, straightlaced, and feared the kinds of experimenting with drugs and encounter groups that my peers were doing, I resolved to expose myself to new ideas and was influenced by many events that expanded my awareness of the issues of the time. I was spellbound hearing Alex Haley speak about his forth-coming book, *Roots: The Saga of an American Family*, and was sobered listening to a talk by a fiery, Black student radical. But for the most part, I kept my head down and studied hard to become a scientist. And it took another ten years before I became as open to new ideas as I was in college.

After earning a bachelor of science degree in biology and a master of science degree in aquatic ecology, I ended up in southeast Alaska studying the effects of logging on salmon streams. I had learned of the fragile state of the world's ecosystems in graduate school and was yearning to make a positive difference. But after six years of field work, I became disillusioned about this endeavor making any differ-ence at all.

In 1982 at the age of thirty-two, I left this job and my known life, packed up my car, and went on the road. I figured I could live on my savings for at least two years if I was frugal. I was deeply discouraged, lacked confidence in myself, and was frustrated that my efforts weren't making any difference. I didn't know what to do next—I just knew that I was dissatisfied with my status quo and wanted something more. This took courage and faith that I would uncover what my life was to be about. At the time, I had *no idea*. But something was brewing within: a pull to discover more dimensions of myself in addition to the scientist and nature lover.

I camped and hiked in the national parks all over the United States while beginning to explore my inner realms, awaken my spiritual being, and try to figure out a path forward. I read lots of self-help and spiritual books, searching for that something more. I got inklings here and there, but had no notion of how to live it or what my life might look like.

Chapter 2

Dinosaur National Monument: Meeting the UV Family

It was a year and a half into my travels that I met Evy on that trail in Dinosaur National Monument and said yes to meeting her friends. She commented that I wouldn't have trouble finding them because their motor home looked like a bread truck. Later, as I walked through the campground, it was easy to spot—an ivory-colored step van with a curious upper story and solar panels on the roof.

Evy was waiting for me and invited me in. A wiry, pipe-smoking Latino rose from the driver's seat, saying, "Hi, I'm Joe." Next I was drawn to the left, where Monica introduced herself, exuding a warmth like the mother most of us wish for and never had. She was short and energetic, with dark hair and kind eyes. As I looked around, I saw an opening in the roof leading to the upper story. A friendly, curious face poked down to say hi—it was Vicki.

Long, vinyl-cushioned seats lined both sides of the front of the vehicle. The back part of the van was a kitchen space with a sink, a range, an oven, and a refrigerator. Most of the walls contained storage units, and there was a wall of books behind one of the long seats. But this was not your ordinary motor home. Evy had told me that they had designed and built it themselves. A hydraulic lift rose through the access hole in the roof, providing an elegant method of raising the upper story for sleeping and collapsing it to lie flat for travel. Later I would discover for myself that you had to be something of a gymnast to climb up there, but even Evy had found her own unique way of hoisting herself up. It was like being in a tree house above the ordinary world.

I couldn't spend much time taking in the scene because I was immediately drawn into conversation. When they asked me about myself, they listened intently, asking probing but respectful questions that took me deeper into my current angst, hopes, and dreams. About this time, Vicki came down to join us, realizing that there was something more important happening than the project she was working on.

As a woman traveling alone, I was always wary, looking for anything that might be a threat to my safety and well-being. In this case, I wondered if they were what at the time were called Jesus freaks because they seemed to be living what Jesus preached more than anyone I had ever met. Were they trying to recruit me? But the warm, embracing welcome; the sincere questions; and the lightheartedness and laughter that interspersed the conversation allowed me to relax.

As the evening wore on, my excitement grew. This strangely compelling group of people were living their values and working to *save the world* (that is, make the world a better place). They engaged me about where I was in my life while at the same time painting a picture of what could be, how *I* could be, how the *world* could be. They were speaking to my Larger Self about a way of living that I could imagine stepping into. I was already partway there and just needed the inspiration, their example, and the recognition that it was possible. At some unconscious level, I had been yearning for that ever since high school. I had sensed it, but now I was being given the permission and urging I needed.

I found out soon enough that they espoused no one spiritual path, allaying my concerns about being recruited. Above the driver's seat, Joe had on display a rotating collection of photos of his gurus that included Monica, Jesus, an Indian guru named Swami Satchidananda, and a chimpanzee. Their happiness, lovingness, and acceptance of a stranger like me, as well as their passion for life and the world, rekindled my lost idealism. Here were people living their ideals and contributing to making the world a better place—something that had eluded me so far. I knew they knew something that I wanted to know, and I caught their spark and vision.

At their urging, I spent the next two days with them before they continued west and I continued east. I learned the basics of their story.

Joe and Monica had been beatniks living together in New York City and part of the countercultural movement of the 1960s. Joe had grown up in Spanish Harlem and was a former Wall Street technical analyst. Monica had been a book editor in the city and ended up editing Joe's weekly stock market letter and being his assistant in technical analysis. They had both saved enough money to become financially self-sufficient following a plan that Joe had developed for himself that did not involve investing in the stock market. In 1969, at thirty years of age, they left New York City, thinking they were on their way around the world. They stopped at spiritual centers and communes as they drove across the country, but no teacher or commune was so compelling that they wanted to interrupt their journey.

Monica reflects on that time period:

Joe and I were on a journey we didn't know exactly how to name, look-ing for something else, on the road to explore life. I had a desire and an awareness that there was something more to life that began when I was still in college. And there had been something internal driving Joe well before leaving New York, some force that was really strong. "There's something just beyond my grasp," he'd say. "I can see it. I can feel it."

Vicki and her then-husband, Mark, both in their early twenties, also left New York City in 1969. Their aspirations in the entertain-ment world had never quite panned out. So one day, they put all their furniture out on the sidewalk, bought a four-wheel drive sta-tion wagon, got a dog from the pound, and started a cross-country adventure. They *thought* they were on their way to Tierra del Fuego at the tip of South America, driving the partially completed Pan-American Highway.

A year later, both couples ended up in the same campground in Mazatlan, Mexico. As they shared their yearning for a life of meaning and happiness, they immediately felt a kinship with one another. Because of the quality of their explorations and the aliveness they all felt in Mazatlan, they decided to stay together for a while. This was the beginning of what they later called a Grand Adventure. They rented a house at the edge of a remote, Mexican fishing village without electricity, where they were out of the mainstream and away from all that was familiar. They thought they would try it for a couple of weeks but stayed for one and a half years.

In a quest for internal freedom and an intense desire to learn how life really worked, they created their own little society. They realized that everything they'd been told about how life worked might not be true. So they put themselves through self-directed training in deconstructing the Western mindset through inquiry into what was real and what was true. Ritual use of LSD and pot gave them glimpses of a different reality that they wanted to be able to experience and live from when they were not high. They were determined to learn what they could and to grow however they could, to transcend ordinary reality and live something larger. They were experimenting with new ways of being. Some of it was difficult to articulate, so they created an informal lexicon of terms using common language to signify complex ideas or group experiences. Many words and phrases used in this narrative derive from this time in their lives.

Of course their Grand Adventure was a response to the idealistic, we-can-change-the-world times of the late 1960s and early 1970s. Young people were exploring, going on the road, experimenting with drugs, and questioning the system just like these two couples were. Many had been influenced by the spiritual idealism of the American transcendentalists like Ralph Waldo Emerson and Henry David Thoreau. And people wanted to live what they were seeing or glimpsing when they were stoned.

During their time in Mexico, they examined every aspect of their lives to see what was true for them, and they came up with a set of "temporarily valid truths," or principles about how life—or, at least, their lives—worked. Their conclusion was that what makes life worth living was love and service. Now the vision had to be lived.

About this time, a teacher friend visiting from Chicago asked them to come to northern Wisconsin to develop a piece of land he had bought sight unseen. He had a plan to use the land for a halfway house or alternative school for street kids from Chicago. This was a perfect practicum: "Can we city folks live the truth of love while spending our days learning to live on the land—erecting buildings, gardening, and living off the land? Can we make it real?"

Well, they were certainly game to try. So their explorations in Mexico came to an end, and they packed up and headed to Rhinelander, Wisconsin. By this time, Mark had left the core group, but on the way to Wisconsin, two other young people caught their vision and became an integral part of their Rhinelander family.

So the Rhinelander group did the hard work of homesteading, learning how to do it from books, trial and error, and kindly neighbors who took a liking to these strange but friendly hippies. Their spirit of zaniness, adventurousness, and optimism comes through in the book of practical how-tos they compiled during this time that I read many years later. A couple of examples:

Watch out! Hold on! Running your kitchen at Rhinelander may well prove to be a roller-coaster adventure making your city cooking seem like the kiddy choo-choo in comparison. You have no electricity, no running water, no linoleum floor, no sink with mysterious drain pipe leading Chicago-knows-where. As a matter of fact, as of now, you have no kitchen. All you've got is one propane stove sitting in a clearing wrapped up in polyethylene, maybe. And you plan to feed a dozen people three times a day? It may also hold many unexpected natural delights and many real satisfactions. Like everything else at Rhinelander, it can be a focus for awareness, for tuning into yourself and the world around you. An afternoon baking can, if you're open to it, be a sensual delight, or meditation, or total here-nowness.

You drive through the gates over to the building supplies section first. Good, a few 2x4's, some linoleum, and oh look, a whole stack of ceiling tiles. Any automotive goodies today? No? Well, on to housewares and toys. A plastic mixing bowl, and we can always use another chair. What is this? Some far-out department store? A flea market? Nope. This is your local dump.

After three years, they discovered that, indeed, they could live the truth of love in the real world, and the idea of going on the road to be of service was calling them. They wanted to be self-contained so they wouldn't be a burden on the communities and organizations they would be visiting. And their convoy of three old vehicles was impractical and unwieldy.

So they decided to build what they called the Ultimate Vehicle (UV for short)—their motor home—and build it to accommodate six people and last at least twenty years. Over time I would learn about the state-of-the-art materials they had used and the redundancies they had built in so that if one thing broke down, there was another way to fill that need. Everything had to have more than one use. Their values of impeccability and no leeway especially applied to this period, and every step in the building process was done with intention and competence.

The storage spaces inside the step van were constructed of aluminum modules, and each person had one module—a drawer and a cabinet with sliding shelves—for their personal space. Later, the phrase (sometimes said seriously, sometimes jokingly), "Put it in your module," was used to convey that the new item you had just acquired could not be absorbed by the group space, and if you wanted to keep it, it had to fit in your module.

In 1976, they were ready to put their ideals in service to the world. As they traveled in the UV, they visited intentional communities, met people in campgrounds, and volunteered for nonprofit organizations. People started calling them the UV Family after their motor home. They soon discovered that what people really wanted to know was, "Why don't you guys have to work? How come you can live lives of service?" When the UV Family talked about how important financial independence was to being a more effective planetary-change agent, people were eager to learn how to achieve it.

Of course, I wanted to know that too. Later in my two-day visit in Dinosaur National Monument, Joe sat me down to explain how each of them had become financially independent, living frugally on their savings. He had summarized his learnings into a nine-step program that anyone could use for getting one's expenses in line with what provided fulfillment in life, living frugally and ultimately becoming financially self-sufficient, freeing oneself to live a life of service. Already my mind was scheming about how I could become financially independent with the income from the savings I had amassed in Alaska so that I could contribute to making the world a better place. I was glad that I had, on my own, been following some of the recommended steps already.

In 1980, the UV Family took on a yearlong project of setting up local Human Unity groups in twelve western states in preparation for the 8th Annual International Human Unity Conference to be held in Vancouver, British Columbia, in 1981. They traveled to each location, helped establish a group, and then went to the next place. Each group needed funds for organizing. So they created a financial seminar, "Transforming Your Relationship with Money and Achieving Financial Independence," to teach what they knew about how to extricate oneself from an unfulfilling job and accumulating debt, freeing up time for a more meaningful life. They would then donate the proceeds from the seminar to these local groups.

It was at one of these local Human Unity groups, in Tucson, Arizona, that they met Evy. At the time, she was "a bowl of Jell-O in a wheelchair," dying from amyotrophic lateral sclerosis (ALS, or

Lou Gehrig's disease) with less than one year to live. But they found her to be the most vibrant person at the gathering. From her deep soul-searching as she journeyed through illness and faced dying head-on, she had already achieved insights similar to theirs. She was determined, outgoing, and impish, and had a lot of inner power in her small package.

Once they settled in a rented house in Vancouver to work on the conference, they invited Evy to stay with them, and it wasn't long before it became clear that she was no longer dying, but actually improving in physical function. One day, they came home to find her wheelchair on the porch, empty, and Evy taking her first walk down the sidewalk since losing use of her legs early on in her illness. By the time I met her, she had been living and working with the UV Family for several years.

In between visits to intentional communities and service organizations, the UV Family found places to camp where they could recharge themselves, tighten their connections with one another, and begin to articulate what they were learning. During these times, Monica wrote poems and songs, Vicki created cartoons, Joe sat in the driver's seat of the UV and pondered the group's next steps, and Evy began writing her story of how she recovered from ALS.

"Oh, Mighty River"
(Composed and sung by Monica at night while camping on the Poudre River in Colorado)

> *I sit by the river, here in this tent*
> *Stars overhead and Love heaven sent*
> *Sound of the water, the moon in full view*
> *I'm so filled with joy, I want to send it back to you*
> *O-o-o-oh mighty river, send this love on out*
> *O-o-o-oh mighty river, send this love on out*
>
> *Another day here in this glorious place*
> *I feel the power strongly, I can see it's God's face*
> *My cup runneth over, I must send it out*

So I sit and I sing, I cry and I shout
I sing, O-o-o-oh mighty river, send this love on out

Bless the earth and everyone, let the energy run
Bless the earth and everyone, let the energy run
Bless the earth and everyone, let the energy run
Singin' O-o-o-oh mighty river, send this love on out

They had landed in Dinosaur National Monument for a few days to rest and recharge. Now I became their focus. Later, I would learn that as they walked around whatever campground they were in, their inner antennae were out, sensing anyone who might be on a similar path, on a spiritual search, or going through a hard time in their life. If they sensed an opportunity, they would strike up a conversation to see if there was openness to more than a friendly hi. Over time, they started humorously referring to this as *campground ministry*. So I became a grateful recipient of their campground ministry.

I was eager to hear as much as I could during these two short days while we were together. In long walks with Vicki, this attractive, vivacious woman with lively, hazel eyes articulated a compelling vision of a world based on love and service. She conveyed her passion for bringing that about through empowering people to take control of their lives in the areas of finances and relationships. In strolls with Evy, she described her experience of the connection between mind and health and more about the process of her own healing. She attributed her healing to a fundamental shift in how she viewed her body and her life, and to her commitment to serve in the highest way possible, even as she was dying. I was touched deeply by her story. Walking with Monica, I felt her loving embrace. Just by being herself, she was a demonstration of love in action—not a wimpy kind of love, but love as a powerful yet gentle force.

Joe talked about his epiphany that love was not a vector, where Dan Cupid shoots his arrow and you're "in love," but a space—the room of love—that you enter when you have removed your barriers to unconditional love. You are in love with whoever else is in that room. There are no conditions to love when you are in that room. So the question, "How do you live the truth of unconditional love?," had become a quest of theirs, requiring experimentation, missteps, honesty, and commitment to noticing when they had slipped back into the old way of thinking about love and removing those barriers to love.

At some point during their time in Mexico, it seemed natural for the four original explorers to choose sexual expression in relationships that were developing the intimacy that comes from being in the room of love together. In this new society they had been creating day by day, being in the room of love together became a main criterion for starting a sexual relationship. So such a relationship was not based on physical attraction but on this foundation of love.

By the time I met them, they considered themselves a group marriage. The idea of Utopian communities with shared sexuality was not new to them. In fact, Vicki had written a paper in high school on the Oneida Community and was fascinated by the capacity to live in such a complex way. But as Joe said, "We never intended to have a group marriage but to explore the nature of unconditional love." Then, sometime in Mexico, they read Stephen Gaskin's book, *Monday Night Class*, where Gaskin used the term *group marriage*, and they said to one another, "Maybe that's what we're building here." So they started using group marriage to describe the relationship among the four of them.

The second evening, they invited me to join them in a communication ritual that was a cornerstone in their spiritual journey together. They called it Heart Sharing. We sat quietly together, and one by one, we took turns speaking from our hearts and our innermost being—whatever was in our minds and hearts to offer into the space. The rest of us listened deeply as if we were listening to God, without interruption or feedback. I can't remember the content of our sharings, but I know I experienced an intimacy and honesty, and felt I was being fully heard and affirmed in a way I never had before.

I grasped the concepts of a different way of being and living, and I resonated with them, almost like they had been within me all along just waiting to be called out. I also experienced this different way of being by how they related to me, one another, and the world around them. And I got my first taste of what that felt like inside myself. I had an *experience* of love and being loved, not just a concept or wishful thinking about it.

There was the compelling vision Vicki articulated on our walks, there was Monica's loving embrace, there was Evy's Midwestern ease and joshing as well as her comfort with her own disabilities, and there was Joe's charisma, spiritually, and sexually. Each person added an essential piece to the picture that led me then and there to decide to hook my fate with these people.

Normally, I would ponder such a life-changing decision for a long time before acting. But I had experienced their heartbeat, and it resonated deeply within me, like a mother's heartbeat to a baby in the womb, and I wanted it for myself. In the short time we were together, I felt deeply seen and met where I was on the spiritual path. I was accepted and even loved for who I was, and my basic goodness was affirmed.

In my heart, I had already married them—after all, we were in the room of love together! As a symbol and celebration of that, Joe and I made love. I learned from Monica later that the others all sat downstairs in the UV quietly holding us with open hearts, without jealousy. They saw what later they would call the sterling quality that I brought to the experience and felt the beauty of that. Evy wrote this poem during that time:

Here amid the creamy colored mountains
our hearts merged.
Giggling and laughing with splendor
we stepped beyond the horizon
filling our senses with love.
Touching our sacrednesses,
our hearts have become one.

We are joined by the unseeable
with a bond unbreakable.
Your beauty is the fragrant essence
which carries us forth
until our paths entwine once more.

In the room of love with you
Forever – or eternity –
whichever comes first.

I drove away from there with a stash of articles and newsletters they'd written and cassette tapes they had recorded. I was captivated by a vision of living one's ideals, living a life dedicated to harmonious, loving relationships and making the world a better place. My experience with these people answered my quest for how to have a meaningful life and meaningful work, how to live my values, what my purpose was, and what could be a compelling vision for my life. This was a tremendous relief. I was giddy with a combination of excitement, trepidation, inspiration, anticipation, passion, and an inner knowing that my life would never be the same.

My diary describes what this time meant to me: "Without a doubt this has been the most significant, most inspirational experience of my life!" A whole new world had opened up for me. "One heart in four bodies"—that's how I described the UV Family.

I wanted this badly enough to change my life, to have family and friends think I was crazy, and to buckle down in learning to know myself for the first time. I was ready to discover places I had never loved in myself, places where I needed to mature, places where I needed to be open to something new. And I wanted to draw forth my very best—my highest aspirations, my best qualities, my courage, my willingness to step into the unknown, the willingness to feel naked, and the determination to encounter and overcome barriers inside myself.

I was *not* the type of person you would expect to be drawn to these people nor would you expect them to be drawn to me. I was serious, straight-laced, uptight, left-brained logical, and a rule-follower. They were zany, crude-talking, internally free, loving, outrageous, irreverent people who turned accepted wisdom upside down to see it from a new angle. I was an innocent who had never taken drugs and had only two foul words in my vocabulary that I used sparingly. They were seasoned travelers to inner realms I didn't know existed. And they freely used slang and even foul language, and enjoyed not being politically correct. Their motto was, "Make hamburger out of all sacred cows, especially your own." Thus began my training in humor, irreverence, and a sense of the absurd.

As I look back on this "chance" encounter, I realize the trajectory of my life hung by a thread that first evening when Evy had invited me to meet her friends. It would have been so easy, safe, and true to my character to say, "No thanks," and continue on my lonely way. I thank whatever inner prompting or nudge from Spirit pushed me to say that one word—yes.

Chapter 3

Fort Collins: Integration Time

A few months later, I wrapped up my travels and rented an apartment in Fort Collins, Colorado, so that I could begin to integrate what I had learned and experienced from the UV Family in our brief meeting. My whole world had been turned upside down, and I spent the next nine months in contemplation and introspection. The UV Family had laid out a whole new paradigm (a new way of thinking) about how the world works. Now I was in the process of a deep, inner transformation—a basic, radical shift; a fundamental change in consciousness; a shift in who I thought I was (my identity) and how I perceived the world.

I used that time to discover what was important to me and how I wanted to live my life. I wrote: "I have to be myself, not what anyone else wants me to be!" The values I grew up with were as important as ever: honesty, reliability, responsibility, conscientiousness, independence, logic, and common sense. But I wanted to try on for size and develop the capacity for the new ways of thinking and living these folks had discovered for themselves in Mexico.

Chief among these were:

- I am perfect just the way I am.
- I create my own experience of reality.

- I am the source of love. Love doesn't happen to me.
- Happiness and fulfillment come from within.

While all these concepts rang true, they were far from how I had been living my life. I definitely didn't feel perfect. I judged myself mercilessly, and I certainly looked outside myself to find love and happiness.

I was fascinated and envious that they claimed to have figured out the secret of living a happy life. They discovered, as so many wise people through the ages had, that happiness is our natural state. When they told me this at Dinosaur National Monument, a light bulb went on. No matter what was happening in my life, I could still access happiness inside me. I had to choose it. I was serious by nature, and finding my internal switch to activate my more lighthearted and joyful side was going to be a challenge. But I knew where to look for it—not out there, but inside myself. I reminded myself of something Evy had told me: "Every day when you get up, you have the *choice* to be happy and fulfilled that day."

Of course I delved into all the materials the UV Family had given me and learned even more about their lives and their vision. They wrote occasional newsletters, distilling their learnings and describing projects they had come across on their travels. They would send these out to their growing network of friends and colleagues, and give them to folks they met along the way, like me. In one of these newsletters, they wrote, "People often happen into our lives when they are in that crack between realities, and we provide a safe space where the available choices can be seen in perspective." That certainly described me! They were now devoted to meeting and supporting transformation in people's lives from an old paradigm to a new one. I was beginning to get a taste of what this paradigm shift felt and looked like for myself. I felt so lucky to have these wise guides in my life.

Now how was I going to anchor that shift for myself?

I was particularly excited and inspired by a cassette tape of Joe and Monica talking about their experience of transformation during their time in Mexico.

The four of them had stumbled on a daily communication ritual that was essential to their inner explorations. Every evening, they would sit in a circle without clothing, their external nakedness symbolizing their inner nakedness; smoke pot; and review their days' activities, interactions, and thoughts from the perspective provided by this altered state. They could look at the ways they stumbled, with curiosity and freshness instead of shame and judgment. They called it Cosmic Show and Tell (CS&T). It became a primary tool in their search for what was true and real, and for letting go of blocks to living in this new reality they were encountering. Later, they called this ritual Heart Sharing—basically CS&T without smoking pot.

They found that their insights during CS&T were hard to live during the daytime. They called it nighttime truth, daytime forgetting. So they started writing down or tape recording their insights the next day, creating an ongoing collective journal of awareness.

One evening, they had had a particularly powerful CS&T, and there was a build-up of energy and excitement. Later that night, after the influence of the pot had worn off, Joe was lying in a hammock when he had a profound experience of enlightenment, meaning a transformation or waking up to a larger reality. Everything the four of them had been uncovering about how the world really worked had come together into one major insight with many ramifications.

Joe recalls:

I was listening to a tape that had been made a week earlier of us sitting around the dining table talking. I just kept hearing in people's sharings something I couldn't quite put my finger on but seemed very important that I find what it was . . . Suddenly everything that we had been discussing seemed to be falling into place and far beyond. One way to describe the experience: I was waking up, literally waking up as if I had been, for the preceding thirty-one years, in a dream state. Another image was of walking out of, inadvertently tripping out of, a box that I had thought was the world. And as I pick myself up off the ground, I see the walls of the box, and I see this enormous world, which I hadn't known was there. I had thought my world was that box, the limits of my world. And I found the secret passage, the secret doorway, by inadvertently leaning on it, and I fell through. So it was that kind of snap.

I realized that every single moment of my life is the net product of everything that I've ever done in my life. Right now, this moment, is the net result of every single thing that I have done in my life. Now, that's very self-evident, but it was also tremendously important to me because if every other moment created this one, then I am now in the process of creating every other moment. What it meant to me was the realization that I am at source, I am responsible absolutely, for my life and how everything in it turns out because I had this moment. This moment is my manufacturing plant for every other moment in my life.

Lying in that hammock, Joe realized he didn't know how to love, and he didn't know what love was. But then it hit him:

I am the source of love. Love is a space, a room, with no conditions and no direction. Love is inclusive, ever expanding. I'm it! I'm totally responsible for everything I experience. When I got that I was the source of love, then pouring love out in whatever way became abso-lutely fulfilling to me. Expectation of return did not enter the picture. Lots of other stuff was absolutely topsy-turvy from the thinking sys-tem, the concept system, that I had held prior to that.

Joe could clearly see the old paradigm way of thinking and the new paradigm. His goal was to transform himself so that he was living in this new paradigm as much as possible.

From one of their newsletters:

Prior Thinking (Old Paradigm)
- God is out there.
- Heaven is then (i.e., in the future).

- I am a victim of circumstances.
- I have to find love, happiness, and fulfillment "out there."
- I can never be whole or perfect.
- I am run by my emotions.
- My worldview is self-centered.

New Realization (New Paradigm)

- God is within me.
- Heaven is now.
- I create my experience of reality and am responsible for every moment of my life.
- Love, happiness, and fulfillment come from within me.
- I am whole and perfect exactly as I am.
- I simply have emotions and can choose and change them at will.
- My worldview is we-centered.

Monica says of Joe's experience:

It came out of what was happening with all four of us: the explorations, the kind of unedited and open sharing we were doing, the sense of being united in a search for something we all knew was vital. It was as if we had been passing the baton from one to the other, building on each other, and it was Joe's turn. The energy was building; everything was feeding into this inexorable raising of Joe up for his enlightenment experience. Excitement about a vision that we somehow saw of a different way to be. We were going for enlightenment, moving into another reality. And we needed each other— community—to do it because we were building off each other. How to build bridges from those peak experiences so that what we experienced then is not separate from our everyday itchin', scratchin' life. Intensely focused and sincere in a desire to see something more. The sense that we were discovering something, on an edge of discovery of new territory. It was fresh, exploratory.

Joe says:

Over the next bunch of months, the words were put against the experi-ence. Much of our time together would be spent pondering, "Does this fit? How does this fit?" Then, if it seemed to fit, testing it in reality.

Each of them was undergoing a transformation. Monica describes her experience:

Rather than waking up with the kind of a start Joe had, it was much more of a slower dawning of consciousness for me. The bottom-line thing was the experience of "I'm it," whether you want to say, "I'm God," or "I'm totally responsible for my experience of everything that happens in my life." It was getting in touch with a power that was within me, so totally different from the games I had played around "little me," that it was like flipping out of that experience of feeling helpless and powerless and a victim, all that realm of stuff. I can choose at any moment to be an enlightened, loving, transformed being.

In a sense, they became one another's source of enlightenment because when one of them faltered, another was there to pick up the thread and remind them of who they really were. They weren't saints, but that didn't stop them from trying and aspiring to be. They were curious, dogged, able to freely admit mistakes without shame and move on. There was a freshness about their pursuit of truth.

Of course, they weren't the only group discovering these ideas during that period of time, but because of their isolation, they weren't being influenced by other spiritual seekers. And spiritual evolution wasn't a common concept like it is now. When someone visiting them in Mexico played them a cassette tape by spiritual teacher Ram Dass, who had just come back from India, they thought, "That guy is finding out what we're finding out!"

Also, Monica, in particular, had done a lot of reading about psy-chology, consciousness, and Eastern religions. In Mexico, she realized that all she had learned were just intellectual concepts for her—she wasn't living them.

Monica explains:

That was a cornerstone of my experience in Mexico. For the first time in my life, Spirit or consciousness—however you want to say it—became real; I mean, it became part of my life! I had it all separated—Spirit's over here and my life's over here. So in my day-to-day decisions and behavior, I had to learn to put into actual practice all that great stuff that I knew so well and be willing to see the ways I wasn't doing that, that what I thought I knew was very far from what I was living and expressing, what I was putting out to other people.

From the time of his enlightenment experience, Joe's goal was to be able to be high, at will, without drugs. He wanted, he said, "to build bridges between that space of enlightenment and his daily life." For a few months, he was successful, and this new reality galvanized and buoyed him. But in the end, it wasn't enough by itself for him to remain happy and fulfilled.

Joe says:

I realized there was still another step. I had still been running the movie that the pinnacle was this awakening, and what I got was something Buddhists have been saying for thousands of years: "It's absolutely useless unless you share it," that beyond the waking up is a commitment to service. Otherwise, you lose it.

After pondering this, he realized that what was missing was putting this love he was experiencing into the world. There needed to be a service component to keeping the love flowing. About this time, the opportunity to develop the land in Wisconsin presented itself as a way to serve, and they grabbed it.

Starting in 1978, the UV Family was strongly influenced by Werner Erhard and est (erhard seminars training) because he was inviting participants in his personal development workshops to transform how they saw and lived their lives and giving voice to what the UV Family had already discovered. His language thrilled and galvanized them. These aphorisms became some of their favorites:

- "Life works when you choose what you got. Actually, what you got is what you chose. To move on, choose it."
- "If God told you exactly what it was you were to do, you would be happy doing it no matter what it was. What you're doing is what God wants you to do. Be happy."
- "Create a world that works for everyone."
- "Find out what's wanted and needed, and do it."

They urged me to take the basic est training, which I did during my time in Fort Collins. The training was helpful in cementing some of the concepts I had learned from the UV Family already. But I found that my connection and learnings from the UV Family were much more useful and important to me than the est training.

I was thrilled to read a book the UV Family told me about: *Voluntary Simplicity: Toward a Way of Life That Is Outwardly Simple, Inwardly Rich* by Duane Elgin. I resonated with that and felt that was how I had been living (at least the outwardly frugal and simple part, and now I was working on being inwardly rich). Marilyn Ferguson's *The Aquarian Conspiracy: Personal and Social Transformation in Our Time* was another book that helped me see that I was part of a much bigger movement. When the UV Family had read it a couple of years earlier, they had found once again someone giving voice to what they had learned and helping them see that thousands of other people were discovering the new ways of thinking—that is, outside the box of the culture—that they had encountered in Mexico, forming a broad movement devoted to living and thinking in a new way.

My first tangible experience of the audacity and optimism with which the UV Family lived their lives was when I learned that they had rented a house on the coast of California to write three books in three months. I knew that they had been giving seminars on three different topics: "Transforming Your Relationship with Money and Achieving Financial Independence," "A Matter of Life and Death—Assuming Total Responsibility for Your Life," and "Sex, Love, and Relationships—A New Roadmap." Now they intended to write books based on these seminars: one on personal finances (the first draft of what came to be *Your Money or Your Life* many years later), one on Evy's experience with the mind-body connection in healing herself (which she is currently rewriting, referring back to this original draft), and one on relationships (that later became an article called "The Possible Relationship: Basic Principles from an Innovative Relationship" in *In Context* magazine).

I was excited about these books, and I couldn't fathom how four people could expect to write them without help! After my months of integration time in Fort Collins, I was ready to jump in, so I offered to come and assist them for a few weeks. I didn't have a clue as to how I could do so, but I knew I could wash dishes.

When my parents came to visit me before I left Fort Collins, Mom said, with tears in her eyes: "Rhoda, I don't like what you're doing, but I don't have anything better to offer you and I trust you." That was tantamount to a reluctant blessing, and I was grateful for it.

"Capitol Reef"

(By Monica, while driving into Capitol Reef National Park, November 1988)

> *Shuddering and heaving*
> *in orgasmic ecstasy*
> *Earth thrusting herself up,*
> *thudding and groaning,*
> *as she folds back upon herself,*
> *tilts,*
> *and turns inside out*
> *to reveal (to awestruck eyes)*

the stations of time,
records of change.

Tell me about the unyielding solidity of rock!
The winds of countless deserts leave their mark,
ancient seas lie embalmed
and unknown forces deep within
will once again heave and thrust.

Tell me about permanence! . . . eternity!
To see Earth, belly up,
her rocks flung as in some tantrum of ecstasy
and stony reefs tilting crazily like sinking ships,
plunging . . .

If this primal bedrock,
essence below all shifting forms of life,
can twist and turn with such abandon,
what transfigurations await tomorrow?

This, then, is Kali . . .
The fierce wild face of The Mother.

Chapter 4

Jenner: Leaving Barriers at the Door

It was August 1984 when I pulled into the driveway at the house the UV Family had rented near Jenner, California, on a bluff overlooking the Pacific Ocean. I was tired from the long drive and apprehensive about what I was walking into. But the late-afternoon sun sparkling on the lush, green shrubs and pink fuchsia, and the sea breeze with the booming ocean in the background, were soothing, and I was reassured by a joyful welcome from Monica and Vicki.

But a woman named Marcia also greeted me warmly, and I learned that she was staying with them. My first reaction was disappointment that I wouldn't have the UV Family all to myself. And I was concerned about how this new woman and I would relate. When I look back at my possessiveness and lack of inclusiveness and openness, I just laugh because Marcia was to become a strong source of support and friendship over the next few months and was soon just as dear to me as the others. That was my first lesson in how easy it could be to let possessiveness and jealousy rob me of the gifts of inclusivity.

Marcia had been living at Alpha Farm in Deadwood, Oregon, which was one of the intentional communities in the Earth Communities Network (now the Foundation for Intentional Community) that the UV Family visited many times after the Human Unity conference. When they met Marcia, there was a mutual recognition, and the five of them developed a very strong connection. The UV Family described Marcia to me as the "Sufi in the kitchen"—i.e., conveying spiritual wisdom and calm engagement by her very presence as she went about her tasks in the kitchen or garden at Alpha Farm.

The UV Family had spent many years primarily focusing on spiritual exploration and their own spiritual growth. But starting in the early 1980s, their main focus was on putting their ideals in service to the world and offering their wisdom to others through writing and speaking. This shift was catalyzed in part by Werner Erhard's call to be of service in a larger way in his seminar, "A World That Works for Everyone." So when people like me came along who were immature spiritually, we had to do our inner work and learning the art of living a life of love and service in the process of life itself, not as a full-time focus like they did in Mexico. I became an eager student.

During this time in Jenner, the UV Family were not only immersed in writing but were also welcoming me and other visitors. They would take time out to gather in the living room after dinner each evening to tell us what they'd learned about life, spiritual growth, money, relationships, and health. Often, they would use storytelling—both real-life stories and teaching stories—to communicate a concept or experience. "The Jeweled Hallway" is an example of the kind of teaching story they shared during these evenings. I couldn't count the number of times in my life I'd gotten fixated on a "black dot," missing the wonder of this life.

"The Jeweled Hallway" (a teaching story by Joe)

Imagine a long hallway with this wall of absolutely beautiful colored lights, ever-changing, kaleidoscopic. Millions of flashes of light. Every square inch is aglow with this incredible display of color. You're just walking along this hallway, and no two bits are the same—they are always different. Every single bit is absolute perfection.

And as you continue walking down, all of a sudden, you see this tiny, dark spot. And you leap at it, push your nose against it, press your eyeball against it, and you start screaming, "It's dark, it's black, it's black in there! My God, what am I gonna do? It's black! Will somebody

help me? It's black!" You get totally strung out on that tiny little pin-
hole between the colors, and you get stuck there, screaming.

People walk by and say, "Well, move on. If you don't like that dot
of black, move on—there's absolutely no reason to stay there. Look
around you. Look at all these other colors. Life moves on. Just keep on
walking."

While Heart Sharing was not necessarily the nightly spiritual practice it had been for their first ten years together, it was still an important ritual, and we spent many evenings accessing the inner wisdom
available in this kind of sharing.

They also used these evenings to share what they had learned
about relationships, starting all the way back in Mexico. I was glad
to hear more about how their sexual relationships had evolved back
then. Adding new sexual partners in Mexico had opened the territory
of feelings and reactivity. So, in addition to their larger philosophical
discussions, they had needed to process these emotions. Rather than
pulling the group apart, these experiences became fodder for inquiry
and new ways of seeing.

Monica reflects on the time in Mexico:

I became aware of a whole other level, that because we are intercon-
nected, everything we do has an effect in the world – and we usually
don't even know what it is. I realized that this applies to sexual rela-
tionships as well. Everything that two people in a relationship do has
an effect in the world. It became pretty clear that everything we did
in Mexico had an effect in our small universe of four. Now we were
becoming increasingly aware that the effects go out further—we
have no idea of how far the effects go. The enormity of that aware-
ness became a cornerstone in any decision I made, and that's across
the board. I'm talking in terms of a sexual relationship, but it's true of
absolutely everything else I do. Realizing that in making a decision to

come together with someone sexually, I had to follow the ripples out as far as my consciousness could go—all the people that each of us were and are and have been involved with, the people in our immediate environment, the people in the town, the people that are in our lives from the past. I have to be willing to take responsibility for all of that. When I got that's how it worked, that was awesome; discovering that going to bed with someone wasn't a private act—that was a biggie.

They discovered a way to avoid jealousy when one of them wanted to start a sexual relationship with someone outside the group: bring any potential new friendship or sexual relationship home so everyone could be included. Monica made the inner commitment of, "Okay, whomever one of us is sexual with, they are in my heart." This principle of inclusivity became a cornerstone to their expanding sexual relationships. It required stretching themselves to include new people in their love, and it often, although not always, ended up increasing everyone's joy and aliveness.

Sometimes jealousy would still arise. After all, they had been deeply programmed by our culture that it was natural to feel jealous. Especially as the group expanded beyond the original four in Mexico, each new addition, like me, required expanding the boundaries of the group and either whole-heartedly welcoming the newcomer or experiencing the jealousy of having to share their intimate partners with yet another person. I think it was easier for those of us who came along later than for the earlier members, even though they aspired to inclusivity.

Monica reflects on the Mexico experience:

The Grand Adventure really had to do, first and foremost, with the spiritual search. It was an adventure, and it was great. On the form level, we were doing a lot of different things. Sexuality was one of them— open relationships and group marriage, and that community sense of sharing sexuality as well as sharing everything else. That was beautiful to me, even though I had been jealous. What was beautiful about it, I thought—and this was part of the spiritual thing as it seemed to me at the time—was that it was part of the letting go of old strictures and structures, of old constraints that were ego-based: for example, getting over and working through jealousy rather than allowing that to run us. That we were bigger than that. That we could encompass more of the world and make love to it, make love to people we cared about. It was part of the adventure—of trying new things. We were open to new things; we were open to living in different ways. And working together to see how each one of us was needed and had a part to play and didn't feel outside of it.

By this time in Jenner, almost fifteen years since their explorations in Mexico, they were clearer on what made their group marriage work. It entailed a lifetime commitment to one another, but with no particular form. There was a dedication to supporting one another in being their highest selves. The purpose in being together was to put out more love into the world, and group marriage made this more effective than if each person was working separately. Monica says, "Out of two, three, or four people coming together in a relationship, each person being whole and complete, a joining happens that releases something incredibly powerful. Call it cocreative or being together for a higher purpose."

I really bonded with the concept of us as a group marriage. It captured what was true in my heart. But I learned later that not everyone was keen on this term as our group expanded—some preferred *family* to describe this larger entity. In fact, in their Wisconsin days, they had used that term and defined it as "a very tightly knit group, violating societal rules, but with their own definite moral, ethical, and sexual codes."

The UV Family described a powerful image for a solid relationship: a pyramid. Such a relationship was founded on a wide base—alignment at the spiritual part of our being. The layer above this was emotional maturity and then intellectual rapport. Only at the very top of the pyramid was sexual expression. In the old paradigm of relationships, the pyramid was upside down, with sexual attraction forming the basis for starting the relationship, with mental, emotional, and spiritual alignment on top of that. In their thinking, this inverted pyramid was an inherently top-heavy structure that needed artificial props to keep it from toppling, such as having a baby or buying a new house. I was so grateful to be in these relationships based on spiritual, emotional, and intellectual alignment.

There was an intimacy to our days in Jenner, whether it was gathering for lunch and reporting on our work, a spontaneous hug, a deep conversation with someone, or sexual exploration. There was a dynamism, passion, and optimism to our life. There was so much focus on the various writing projects, so many moments of zaniness and laughter, and so much serious inner and outer work. And there were so many friends and colleagues passing through, bringing new perspectives and their own life successes and challenges to share. Two weeks into my stay, I wrote in my journal, "I've met more people who know who they are and where they're headed in the past two weeks than in the first thirty-three years of my life!"

Meanwhile, I found my niche in listening to open-reel tapes of financial seminars that Joe had done to extract the best of his teaching stories on spiritual principles and concepts as they applied to personal finances. Joe wanted to extricate himself from doing the seminars—which had become very popular, with requests from around the world—while still getting his message out about financial independence. His intention was to combine these teachings into a cassette tape course called *Transforming Your Relationship with Money and Achieving Financial Independence*. This tape course would end up being the predecessor to the book *Your Money or Your Life*, coauthored by Joe and Vicki. This book would hit the bookstores eight years later, bringing the message to a much wider audience.

While I would be huddled over the reel-to-reel machine with headphones on in one corner of a garage temporarily converted into office space, Vicki would be in a different corner writing about the financial work or relationships and Evy would be writing about the mind-body-spirit connection while Monica would be editing all of it. Marcia would be off in another corner with her typewriter transcribing insights on relationships from CS&T and Heart Sharing tapes. Meanwhile, Joe would sit in his office (the front seat of the UV) working on turning his seminar talks into a tape course and looking at the big picture of how our work could serve in the world. This was my first taste of synergy, where the combined effect is greater than the sum of the individual actions. More seemed to get done in one day than was humanly possible. Maybe they *could* actually write three books in three months! Oh, and I did my share of the dishes.

It was also in Jenner that New Road Map Foundation (NRM) became an official entity, a nonprofit 501(c)(3) organization—the basket for what the UV Family had to teach about life. It also offered an easier mechanism for distributing money from talks and seminars to worthy nonprofit groups. Vicki says of the decision: "We became an official organization only reluctantly. We were used to a different mode of operating, following where spirit led, unfettered by government regulations." Over the coming years, there were many moments of wistfulness for the freedom and simplicity of the old days before we had become an official entity, when there were no lengthy IRS forms to fill out or limitations on the projects we could support.

When I arrived at the Jenner house, I was determined to leave my internal barriers (my so-called baggage, my ingrained habits and ways of being) at the door and be totally open to a new reality and way of living. I wanted to live an unedited life (i.e., being totally honest and not omitting the hard, ugly, or embarrassing parts), to experience inclusiveness in relationships, and live in the room of love, not just visit it. My heart opened. Being loved and cherished more deeply than I'd ever experienced before, being validated for who I was, and being affirmed as a woman—these experiences opened me to my own capacity for love, both love of myself and love of others. Having meaning and purpose in life and knowing we were making a difference in the world were answers to prayers I didn't even know I had been praying. I felt like I had come home. I had a deep sense of belonging.

One day found me standing on a large rock on a cliff above the sparkling water of the Pacific Ocean having my picture taken in a blue top and flowy skirt, feeling feminine and fetching. I felt happy and was beginning to find love and acceptance for myself and my body. Another day, we videotaped one another in a conversational setting and then played it back to see what we looked like. Seeing myself not as a still object but as an animated human being shattered my previous self-image. I saw a person who looked like someone I would like and enjoy knowing. That was profound.

Then there was the naked lunch, orchestrated for my benefit as a way for me to experience nudity and especially my own naked body as a beautiful and ordinary thing, not something to hide. Remember, I had left my barriers at the door, so I plunged right in. So here I was, eating lunch with six of us sitting around a long dining table on old-fashioned, wooden, straight-backed chairs with plush velvet seats, all stark naked. And we have a picture to prove it.

Close on the heels of these happy scenes came hard learnings about judgment. One day, gentle Monica sat me down and gave me the unwelcome and shocking news that I was being judgmental about some behavior of Joe's I didn't like and about how others weren't obeying my demand that they be quieter when I wanted to sleep. The honeymoon was over, and I had my inner work cut out for me. This was my first experience with tough love, and she delivered it like a samurai. I was a novice spiritually and emotionally—a diamond still very much in the rough. I hadn't had the spiritual boot camp experience that they had put themselves through in Mexico. In fact, they said I was so thin-skinned I probably wouldn't have lasted a week in Mexico, and they were probably right! So I was much better off doing my spiritual work piecemeal like this. I was new to understanding my emotional reactions, and the concepts of how to be a loving human being, while making total sense, were harder to implement than to intellectually understand. I began to seriously examine and question my own behavior. Sometimes confusion took hold. Other times, I would be focused on the tiny, black dot in the jeweled hallway. Fortunately, I had help.

First, there was my newbie pal, Marcia. We were both in an open, spongelike space. And since our personalities and stumbling blocks were very different, we could compare notes and pull each other out of the dark, inner places, helping each other reframe something when we were stuck and reminding the other of her essential goodness and beauty.

One evening, our group sharing focused on the topic, "How to keep *it* going?"—meaning how to keep the passion, happiness, and love going when feeling stuck in a debilitating emotional reaction or a dark mood. Given that we were all committed to getting ourselves (our small, ego selves) out of the way, this was vital. I still have hand-written notes from that evening—they became a lifeline to hang on to when the going was tough. The main message was, "Magnificence is your birthright. It's already within you. You've allowed someone to trigger a reaction in you, but you are the source of your love, happiness, and passion. And you can come up with tools and reminders to help you return to that space when you slip." One tool was what the UV Family called Bummer Catering Service. The idea was that when you are feeling unloved, reach out to do something nice for someone else without expectation of return.

In *On Becoming a Person: A Therapist's View of Psychotherapy*, Carl Rogers said that for a person to grow, they need an environment that provides them with genuineness (openness and self-disclosure), acceptance (being seen with unconditional, positive regard), and empathy (being listened to and understood). The UV Family provided that rich environment for my growth and unfoldment, from the moment I met Evy on the trail, then through letters when we were apart, and then through living with them. And as I grew, I became part of the fertilizer for the growth of those around me. We all had a chance to thrive and blossom in this garden that was being constantly seeded, tilled, and watered by genuineness, acceptance, and empathy.

As I look back on those months, I see that Marcia and I played essential roles in the creation of our larger family by coming to Jenner in such an open space. Marcia empowered the four of them by embracing their spiritual concepts even though she had been working on her own spiritual development for years. And I remember long walks with Vicki where she would describe the Grand Adventure part of their story, and I would be inspired by all of it, saying *yes!* Then, over time, when one or another of them might be faltering, I would hold them to their ideals, saying, "This is what I learned from you! You taught me this." Vicki said later that my being a fresh person on the scene and asking these questions and exploring this territory reminded her of why she was there, of her ideals, at a time that was particularly difficult in her own spiritual journey.

The few weeks I had intended to stay had extended to a couple of months, and by then, I decided to cast my lot with these people for the long haul. I was so inspired by what I had learned of their lives up to now and was ready to drop everything to join them in trying to live the visions and ideals they had laid out of this alternate reality. As I would discover only many years later, the stories they told about their Grand Adventure, through their evening sharings, their writings, and the UV Family slideshow that documented their lives together, while true in describing their great mythic adventure, ignored the fullness of what they had actually lived. What I heard was the collective narrative, not exactly what any individual experienced. Their more complex reality had its shadow sides and dysfunctions, which I, in my innocence, excitement, and idealism, was ignorant of or not privy to. It wasn't that they deliberately withheld the hard parts so much as they were also invested in, or blinded by, the myth. As our time in Jenner came to a close, this idealized vision of an alternate reality of unconditional love and service shone with a glow that was irresistible. And in fact, I am not sorry that the nuances and shadows were invisible to me because this left me free to bond with the beautiful vision and try my best to live it.

I had already saved enough money from my job in Alaska to place it in safe, high-interest investments and live off the interest if I lived very frugally. I was certainly motivated. I felt like I and we were ordained for something great. I felt a sense of destiny, a call to greatness, a high calling, and I was meant to be a part of that. While that may have been grandiose and wishful thinking, that feeling provided motivation to stick with it when the going got tough—and tougher, as you will see.

Chapter 5

In the UV and Seattle: The Challenges

1985 found me living in the UV with the other four. It sounded so romantic—we were going on the road and then parking in the driveway of the organization we intended to work with. There was the simplicity of the space and possessions and life. But I came into the family with plenty of emotional baggage. Imagine five people living and working in a space the size of a bread truck. Nothing goes unnoticed. There is no privacy. Emotional upsets just sit there and fester if you don't know how to work through them. One woman who was visiting the four of them in the UV before my time said, "I've wondered what your spiritual path was, and now I know —living in an aluminum pressure cooker." Well, pent-up emotions that I didn't know how to process or express built to the point of exploding in this pressure cooker, and it was not pretty.

Ironically, the five of us living in the UV at the time were writing the article "The Possible Relationship" for *In Context* magazine. I sobbed as I told Joe that I wasn't living this *possible relationship* we professed to be living. His response was that our relationship was perfect as it was because I had the inner commitment to work through the hard places and I was of goodwill.

In "The Possible Relationship," the UV Family laid out the underlying principles that made their relationship and group marriage work. In addition to living unedited lives and being in the space of unconditional love, a purpose outside their relationship and service were the ways to make their relationship thrive. An important part of what made their relationship work was alignment at all levels of the pyramid, as I learned about in Jenner. So rather than a relationship based on sexual attraction, theirs was based on shared purpose, a common spiritual foundation, and compatible emotional and intellectual levels. Sexual expression then became a celebration of an alignment at all these other levels. If someone new entered their lives (like me or Marcia), their primary relationship needed to be solid enough to include this other person in their intimacy. The principles in this article were meant to inspire others to create their own possible relationship—not to use ours as a template, but to apply the principles to their own life situation.

Mercifully for me, this period of living in the UV pressure cooker came to an end after several months. We moved to Seattle and rented a real house, with ample space for me to sort through my internal baggage, angst, and confusion. But even that got too cozy for me. Rather than enjoying the energy of the *we*, I felt like I was being pummeled by a whirlwind of activity created by other people.

At their suggestion, I drove to Coos Bay, Oregon, to take a week-long Personal Power workshop at the Ken Keyes Center. This was a turning point for me in seeing how I was not being at choice in my life (being buffeted about and feeling powerless by others' choices) and ways I was giving my power away, especially with my propensity to judge others. I came back from this with the mantra, "Love is more important than being right."

Still, I was needing space to sort out who I had become and what *my* truth was, separate from the bigger *we* I had become a part of. So I rented a room in a rooming house for a few months. Around this time, I attended a conference where we were invited to "turn," like a Sufi whirling dervish might turn. As I did this, I found myself literally at the center of my own whirlwind, creating it as I went. This was a powerful experience of cementing in me the knowledge of my own power.

Around this time, Vicki wrote me a loving, kick-in-the-pants letter in response to my blaming others for how out of control my life seemed:

You have created us. You have drawn us together. That is our purpose for being here. We are your limbs, your servants. That is the reality. You are not fitting into something that was here before. This is all your made-up stuff. Every day, we are creating what you want to create. Each of us take our instructions from you; you are the center of this thing, the leader. If there is something amiss in your creation, you can certainly shift things. Nothing is going on here that is out of your control; if need be, you can correct it. THERE IS NO LITTLE YOU!

These words allowed me to reach once again for the precious vision of each of us being creators of our world and thus cocreators together. She was making the metaphorical point that we were each leading this group, creating it as we went along. I had felt caught up in everyone else's center as if I had no center of my own, but she reminded me that I was just as important in what we were creating as everyone else.

In this spacious separation, and with the help of my friends, I once again found my center, the place inside where I was the creator of my world, the center of *my* whirlwind and not a victim of others' whirlwinds. And I found myself wanting to cast my lot with these people again and do what it took to stay centered and happy. That would be a constant challenge for me, and my diary is full of my agonized efforts to re-right myself when I would become reactive and unhappy.

In many ways, I was ill-suited for communal living because I had needs that weren't easily met in community. I needed lots of quiet, time in nature, more sleep than most, and lots of alone time to process my feelings, remind myself of the spiritual truths I wanted to be living, and find my center. Also, I was sensitive to disharmony, both between others and with others. Oh, and I was ultra-sensitive to noise. But my needs, although not adequately met, were not enough to deter me from this family. Having love, intimacy, purpose in life, meaningful work, and synergy more than compensated for these challenges. The heartbeat was calling me once again.

Part II

The New Road Map Foundation: A Well-Oiled Machine

Chapter 6

The New Road Map Foundation

Finding a House

I wasn't the only one hearing that heartbeat calling. By this time (1986), a community of people committed to this journey had grown around the four core members, including two who lived in Seattle. Marilynn was already part of the larger extended family, having met the UV Family in their Rhinelander days. Also, when Marcia left Jenner, she moved in with Marilynn. They were both working their way toward financial independence and eager to participate more with the UV Family.

The need for a central location bigger and more stable than a motor home became increasingly apparent. In addition to the need for space for more people, there was also a developing need for space for two projects: First, we were about to finish the master for the cassette tape course to replace the live financial seminar, and we needed space to duplicate the tapes and assemble and ship these courses ourselves. Second, Evy and two medical colleagues in Seattle were inspired to do a medical research study, called the ALS Project, studying the mind/body connection in patients with ALS. They would need space for file cabinets and a desktop computer capable of doing statistical analyses. (At the time, IBM PCs were relatively new and more cumbersome than today.)

So we set about finding the perfect house in Seattle that met our list of criteria—the number of bedrooms and baths we needed, a big living room, plenty of workspace, what neighborhoods would work best for us, parking, and what rental price we could afford. Vicki and Monica, our main scouts, looked at dozens of houses, but nothing seemed to gel. In their experience, when it seems like you're pushing the river, then something must not be clear. They looked again at their criteria. About this time, Marilynn, who had been soul-searching about whether she wanted to live with this group or maintain her independence in her own house, decided to take the leap of living with the rest of us. This was the missing ingredient, and the house was found almost immediately, in a quiet neighborhood in northeast Seattle.

When we moved in, we would have been surprised if someone had told us we would be there for the next eighteen years. Of course, this was a new form of the aluminum pressure cooker. As Vicki put it, "If you put a group of people together, the natural conflict of personalities will surface those impurities in your being that need to be seen and dealt with. It's constant spiritual training."

Others Join

Over time, three other people joined our crew—Paula, Diane, and Lynn—so there were eventually nine of us living in the house and one living nearby, with all ten of us working together during the day. Paula met Marcia and me at a small gathering where Ram Dass was posing the idea of a Seattle chapter of the Seva Foundation, a service organization that he was instrumental in creating. There was a mutual recognition among the three of us in our desire to be of service. Diane had often sought out the UV Family when they had found themselves at the same events in the Bay Area where Diane had then lived, and over time, that developed into a friendship. Lynn and her then-husband met the UV Family through a mutual friend. Lynn was at a turning point in her life and was drawn to what they were teaching, especially about financial independence and relationships.

What was so compelling to each of us that we wanted to leave our previous lives and join this group? What were we responding to? Something in our souls said yes to this life. In one way or another, we were each responding to the group heartbeat and the experience of unconditional love. But what did we really say yes to?

Actually, the doorways in were as varied as we were: spiritual seeking, sex, relationships, service, meaning, financial independence, love. But no matter what doorway had led us to this family, we were invited into a process that included spiritual growth, sexuality, service to the world, financial independence, cultivating relationships, cocreation, and community living.

Back in Rhinelander, Marilynn had resonated with the UV Family's nondogmatic spirituality and their unconditional acceptance of her as she was. When she moved into this house, she was saying yes to group marriage.

For Marcia, it was about living a life of love.

For me, the vision was the possibility of beginning to live as one world, one family. I held our lives as a possibility, a beginning for something much greater. I set aside what I had been told all my life and began to experiment, breaking through my Midwestern life into incredible possibility. I broke out of a hard shell, I broke through, and my heart expanded . . . The thing that brought me to endure, even though it got less and less and less as we went on, is that I resonated and loved the idea of being this little group that was a potential nucleus of people living inclusively, a demonstration that the world could be one family.

Diane was saying yes to adventure and to a knowingness that being in relationship with the UV Family was right. For Paula, the most important aspect was our holding up the ideal of life being about giving to the world. For Lynn, Joe shone the light of love on her in a way no one ever had, and that was healing. She was also drawn in by the vision Joe articulated.

For me, the doorway in was the vision of living a life of high ideals, a life of meaning. I said yes to the ideals of total honesty, commitment to one another for life, a purpose larger than myself, living in the space of love, commitment to spiritual growth, inclusiveness, and sexuality as celebration and expression of the divine.

Our ideals were key. Wanting to save the world. Wanting to be of service. Wanting to live our values. There was always the sweet possibility, the vision.

We were all committed to one another. Some of us felt comfortable calling this a group marriage, others called it family. I considered it a group marriage and that I had nine primary relationships. Each of those relationships was unique; some included a sexual component, and others didn't. Those of us who weren't sexually involved still had deep, intimate relationships with one another. One way to say it is that each relationship had its special qualities. For some, that included sexuality. For others, it didn't.

Where Were All the Men? And the Children?

You might legitimately ask, "Where were all the men?" After all, nine women and one man is a provocative combination. In the Rhinelander homesteading days, there were three women and two men. But starting with me and Marcia in Jenner, it was women who were drawn to commit to this group and the vision. It seemed to happen organically. In part, this may have reflected the fact that men in those days were not as drawn to the spiritual search or as willing to grow spiritually as women. In large part, it may have been a consequence of Joe's strong personality—if you were a man, you had to be strong in yourself to want to be in his orbit. There were many men in our larger circle that we all (including Joe) loved and cared about; they were just not living and working with us on a daily basis. Some of these men were in our sexual circle.

You may also ask, "Where were the children?" Unlike many intentional communities, there were no children living with us. Marcia was the only one with children, and they were all grown, leading their own lives. Most of us had made a conscious decision not to have children long before joining this group, either because we didn't feel called to have children or out of a desire not to add to the overpopulation on the planet. We were glad to have our focus be on our larger purpose and not be distracted by raising children. Clearly, children are an essential part of many communities, but not of ours.

A Container Infused with Love: Our House and Backyard

The first thing you saw when you walked into our house was a tall, four-panel, elegant, Japanese screen. You might reasonably have asked, "This, in a household devoted to frugal living?" But it set a beautiful, simple tone. The screen belonged to Marilynn; the wife of a top executive at Boeing had given it to her while she was their cook and working toward financial independence.

Walking into the large living/dining room, you would have seen the old, flowered sofa. It was a bit worn, but I loved it—its pastel flowers with a beige background were lovely to look at, and it was soft and comfortable. I couldn't tell you how many hours I logged in on that sofa. An interviewer for a magazine article commented that it looked shabby and second-hand, which it probably did. We had various other easy chairs and recliners in a circle to create a homey atmosphere where many people could sit together. Beyond this seating area was a long dining room table that could accommodate fourteen or more people if needed.

Sometimes a guest commented that something felt different when they walked into our house—an ambience of encompassment and purpose, a palpable energy field. There was a different spirit afoot, and they liked the feeling. I think they were tuning into the heartbeat of our family.

As you walked out of the living room, you encountered the pass-through and kitchen. In some respects, the pass-through was the hub of the house. Physically, it was a counter between the kitchen and the hallway that led to the living room, the phone and calendar nook, and office spaces. In practice, it was the watering hole, the spontaneous gathering place. We were a snacking bunch, so we were in and out of the kitchen. There was lots of cooking and cleanup to do too. So anyone passing by in the hallway could get happily (or not) sidetracked by a conversation already under way in the kitchen or by someone who wanted to start one. As more people passed by, the participation and congestion grew. If that counter could talk, it would have a lot to say about this family.

The living/dining room, kitchen, and front bathroom were the public rooms. The rest of this rambling, thirty-two-hundred-square-foot, two-story house was offices, bedrooms, and storage areas. The second floor was all bedrooms.

If you took the stairs down to our mostly finished basement, you entered a narrow hallway jammed with cabinets and boxes housing office supplies and the substantial literature we often shared with other people: brochures, booklets, workbooks, and cassette tapes of our own creation, plus literature from our favorite organizations and people. It was a rare guest who left without a little stack of reading material or cassette tapes.

Farther on was a large room filled with used ophthalmic equipment, of all things. For many years, I was head of the Seattle Seva Eye Project, a subproject inspired by that gathering with Ram Dass where we met Paula. This equipment would be assessed, cataloged, and appraised by a local ophthalmologist, then boxed up and flown to Kathmandu, Nepal, at no cost by Thai Airways in Seattle. It would be used to help eliminate blindness in that country where blindness from cataracts was common. Through the years, thirty-three ophthalmologists donated equipment and supplies valued at over $100,000.

This was also the windowless room where we assembled the cassette tape courses, a hundred at a time. An elf-size door on a wall above a counter led to the Annex, a crawl-in space that was our main storage area for boxes of literature. You couldn't stand up straight in there, and it was back-breaking work keeping that space organized and usable. I rammed my head on the treacherous beams too many times to count.

The basement also housed an office, a bedroom, a shop, and another storage area that was equally difficult to access.

Our backyard sometimes became public space too. It housed the UV, but your gaze would be drawn to the two special trees. One was a tall, Siberian elm that towered above the yard and house, and was a neighborhood landmark. The other was the fig tree. This graceful tree with its plate-size leaves provided the best shade in our yard and embodied the soul of our family. Its broad embrace and protective presence provided the heart and hearth with which we tried to welcome all visitors. Many an hour we spent sitting under its capacious arms. On most summer evenings, we'd eat at the picnic table under the tree.

If you walked around our yard, you'd see small strips of garden where vegetables or flowers were planted. Unlike many intentional communities, we didn't grow much of our own food. We were simply focused elsewhere. In the last few years of our time together, an avid gardener came into our lives and planted bountiful gardens on our parking strips, demonstrating how much produce could be grown with the kind of commitment and love she brought to that endeavor.

Our house and yard provided a container for us and our work, and we infused them with love.

A Day in the Life of NRM

The day began early at the intentional community that by now was known as the New Road Map Foundation or NRM, after our nonprofit name. By 5am, Evy would be silently talking to God and writing in her journal in the front office. Little did we or Evy know that she would one day become a Methodist minister.

Next you'd find Vicki sitting by the window in her basement office with a stack of Post-its. No sooner had she sat down than ten different creative ideas arrived, and the Post-its would be flying. After a while, she'd happily start her daily round of networking and phone calls with her publicist, friends, and colleagues, and capturing ideas from her Post-its on the computer. Sometimes she and Marcia would spend an hour sitting in front of our living room windows, looking out over the Cascade Mountains and reflecting on their lives and the world together. Marcia remembers that time as being very carefully carved out and precious. If Marcia wasn't doing that, she might have gone for a walk, cleaned up the kitchen, or answered the phones, which were often already ringing. She had long since done her morning meditation in her room. Monica would have had coffee and then gone out to the UV to meditate.

Now Marilynn would be sitting at her spot on a stump in the backyard under the fig tree, quietly and reverently greeting the day, not with words but with her whole being. She didn't know yet that she would be drawn to Native American spirituality. I'd groggily wake up to my alarm clock, wanting to do my centering prayer (a form of Christian meditation) in my room and have breakfast before our 9am gathering. I'd be in my own quiet space and tried to be invisible in the kitchen and return to my room as soon as I could to eat my breakfast alone. Now Diane and Lynn would slowly feel their way into the day. And by 9am, Joe, our night owl, was usually up and drinking his tea and having a smoke.

Then we'd all meet for our morning gathering. After all the hugs and greeting one another, we'd start by each giving a short (or sometimes long) "weather report," checking in with anything a person wanted to say about their current state—mental, physical, emotional, or spiritual. One person might have been struggling with anger, another with a painful back, and someone else could be feeling joyful or enthusiastic about something they had heard or read. The rest of us would listen with compassion and openness as each person spoke. Sometimes Joe would have some article in hand that he had read late the night before, ready to share his insights about what it might mean for our work.

We'd talk about the choreography of our day—what needed to be done, what we wanted to achieve, or what guests might be coming. We'd make our plans, knowing that the Universe might give us different "dancing lessons from God" (a phrase coined by Kurt Vonnegut) than we expected. For example, something unforeseen might happen to change the whole trajectory of the day. Sometimes our gathering was short, and sometimes it went on and on for a few hours as we grappled with hard emotions or complex decisions about our work. At its best, we would all leave feeling more connected and clearer about how our day would unfold in harmony and united in purpose with everyone else's. At its worst, it was a grueling exercise in patience as we tried to reach a consensus on some sticky issue, either personal or work-related. Then we'd have to remind ourselves why we were there and why this was important—that something larger that was pulling us.

Now, here's the thing: instead of sitting at a table with our coffee, we sat in a circle on pillows on the floor of one of the bedrooms, all naked. This might sound quirky, but experience had shown the group that we could be more honest and vulnerable without being able to hide behind clothes. And of course this tradition went all the way back to Mexico days. Our goal was to live unedited lives with one another, and our morning gathering was a place to practice that.

The morning gathering started out being more of a personal check-in and less of a business meeting. But as our outer work became the dominant part of our days, it also dominated this gathering. The morning the first copy of our book on personal finances, *Your Money or Your Life*, was delivered and brought into our gathering, we oohed and aahed at what we had done. For Marcia, that experience was burned into her brain. During the months of the publicity tour, this gathering took on a surreal quality. Imagine Vicki taking a call from *The Oprah Winfrey Show* stark naked.

After this gathering, we would disperse to do whatever we had decided our day would be about. This could include the following:

- Household chores: There was no chore wheel; we each saw different things that needed to be done, figured out what was ours to do, and did it. In addition to the daily and weekly chores, Vicki repaired the chimney and cleaned it, I took on controlling the yellow jackets and scraping moss off the roof, Vicki and I learned about the heating system, Joe did bike repair, Evy and Marilynn stockpiled emergency food and water, and Monica planted a garden—all in the process of life itself. If each of us took on the things we saw and did them with joy and equanimity instead of resenting the time it took away from the so-called real work, then home-owning didn't seem like a chore and we would have a supportive, well-functioning shelter for the work that we did.
- Our personal maintenance, like exercise: walking, jogging, yoga, aikido, or biking.
- Times together in pairs devoted to strengthening and deepening each of our connections with every other

person in the group. This might be sexual time, walking in the neighborhood or on the bike trail and having a lively conversation, or going to the arboretum or beach if there was enough time.

- Errands, both personal and for the house.
- Database management and fulfilling tape course orders.
- Correspondence with people interested in our work (by hand, electronic typewriter, or computer—no email back then).
- Answering the phone and responding to people's inquiries about our work.
- Preparing talks or writing articles, newsletters, or our book.
- Kitchen management and cooking.
- Doing data processing for the ALS Project and planning for the next round of patient testing.

At noon, a contingent led by Joe and Marilynn bicycled to the post office to pick up the day's mail, including orders for our tape course. This was a jovial, fun, and sometimes ridiculous-looking event as this parade of maybe six bicycles, including an adult tricycle when Evy joined them, headed to the post office. Joe livened things up by clowning around. It was a way to be outside, get exercise, and have some fun, even though only one person was really needed to pick up the mail.

For the rest of the day, the house would be humming with activity. You'd likely find Monica and Vicki in their shared downstairs office—Monica busy editing or writing letters and Vicki on the phone. Marcia would be answering the other phone line, while a volunteer was working in the back room. Joe and Marilynn would be filling orders for the tape course in the back room, and I might be in the computer closet doing statistics on the ALS Project. Diane might be working on a computer database, and Lynn might be on yet another computer. Paula might be writing or editing a piece for one of our newsletters. Whoever had spare time would be cleaning up the kitchen or perhaps visiting with guests in the living room.

By late afternoon, Evy or Marilynn would be in the kitchen preparing dinner for at least ten people, often twelve or fourteen. Mealtimes were about conviviality and simple but tasty food. They were often joyful, engaging, and stimulating.

We could be as humorous and fun-filled as we could be focused and intentional. Puns, quips, and making fun of ourselves provided occasions for raucous laughter. Because some of us were slower to catch on to the pun or joke, there would be delayed laughter, which would initiate another round of belly laughs, leading to more rolling laughter. This provided a much-needed break from the intensity and seriousness of our lives. To this day, all one of us has to say is a word or phrase to conjure up the whole event and elicit laughter even after so many years have passed.

We would often invite guests for dinner, with the evening devoted to explorations, drawing out our guests, and discourse by our most articulate spokespeople—Joe, Vicki, or Evy. Topics dear to our hearts included the spiritual path, love, relationships, personal finances, the economy, and the relationship between mind and body in health. Sometimes these discussions went late into the night, with us early birds quietly slipping out and heading off to bed. If the guests left by 10pm or so, we would all gather to handle any business that needed to be done from the day and to catch one another up on the day's activities. For example, Marcia might report on a phone call from someone who had been influenced by the nine-step program. Paula might have come across a useful article in a magazine she was reading. Or Vicki might have had a great idea about how to reach more people with the financial work. I would be tired by this time and remind myself that these meetings were important to maintain our smoothly operating system and synergy. Sometimes it was truly inspiring how much the ten of us accomplished in one day, even if my piece seemed like peanuts. That was the power of synergy.

After everyone had a turn to report on any business or news they had, some of us would drag off to bed, while some of the night owls "gorked," which involved watching something taped from TV that didn't necessarily have any redeeming value. Others would go off to their rooms or offices to wind down and take stock of the day's activities.

Once a week, we would have Family Night, an evening of Heart Sharing. Because everyone was encouraged to talk until they had said everything they needed to say, these evenings could be three- or four-hour marathons. One person might share their perspective about an event in the past week that illuminated something for me. Another person might be feeling depressed or discouraged, and I would feel compassion for them. Someone else might talk at length about some aspect of the spiritual journey or relationships that added a new dimension for me. By the end of the evening, we all felt more connected and a part of this larger picture we'd just painted. Marcia noted, "Heart Sharing is one time when I feel totally present because we have an agreement that we are listening to the voice of God within each one of us."

While we were each financially independent, we did have joint expenses that we each contributed to, such as food, utilities, repairs, and large purchases. Everyone paid rent, apportioned according to their means and whether they had their own room or not. This was not a science, but a right-brain process. For example, because of my low monthly income, I paid less rent. It was worth it to the others to subsidize me so I didn't have to get a job that would take me away from the work we were doing. If there was any grumbling about this, I never heard it. And I was grateful not to have to return to work.

Vicki came up with a metaphor for our community. From one vantage point, we were like the crew of the *Starship Enterprise*, going where no one has ever gone before. From another, we were a monastery, living our lives according to the will of Spirit. This intentional community really was some amalgam of the two, an entity much larger, more effective in the world and more tuned in to Spirit than any one of us alone could ever have been. Perhaps it was this, more than anything, that kept us hanging in there when we were tired, when the going got tough, when we didn't really want to do what was on our plate for the day. I held on doggedly to this sweet vision and was totally hooked on the synergy that we created.

Well, and that we loved one another—or tried our best to. In our hearts, we'd committed to that. Staying in love with nine other people with whom you lived and worked was a spiritual practice all by itself and was not for the faint of heart. It required self-examination, self-understanding, willingness to get past the stuck places, and commitment to leaping back into the space of love as soon as one could manage it. Sometimes it was excruciating; sometimes humbling; occasionally, it was easy to turn the heart back toward love. It required reaching inside for one's highest self and giving more weight to that self than the ego. Unconditional love was our aspiration. I personally was grateful to be able to be loving most of the time, even if lurking in the background there were conditions I placed on that love.

But keeping the love lines open among every other person in the community was a priority and took constant vigilance. We wanted the depth of love that we saw in some married couples or in the Mother Teresas of the world. It was a tall order to keep this kind of love flowing while running a foundation, writing our book on personal finances, and conducting a medical research project.

Vision, ideals, synergy, and love—a Grand Adventure indeed.

Friends and Colleagues

Our friends and colleagues were a vital part of our community. There were many avenues by which friends entered our lives. Sometimes it was a person one of us encountered in our daily life or through another organization we were a part of—perhaps there was a spark of recognition or a sense that there was more to do together. Many were seekers on their own spiritual journey, others were interested in our financial program, and still others wanted to talk about relationship issues or alternative lifestyles. Many of the more than two hundred volunteers who worked with us over the years became friends.

One-on-one times outside our main group, perhaps during a walk or sitting at a café, were enriching and brought us fresh ideas and ways of being. Through these interactions, both parties might be changed. On my many walks and talks with our various friends and colleagues, I would often be influenced by a penetrating question, an insight, or a revelation that spoke to a place inside of me.

One day, a young woman who regularly shared her journey of transformation with us described the ritual she had just done to marry herself, an important step on her path of self-love, self-acceptance, and self-respect. She opened my eyes to how I might find/declare that inner marriage for myself.

Sometimes a friend was dealing with an issue that I might encounter later in my own life. For a few years, I volunteered with Beyond War (an organization seeking to build a world without war), and Marcia and I were part of a sharing circle of six women from this group. I had long walks with one of these women, who was a powerful leader in Beyond War. After many years of fulfilling work, she was questioning her role in the organization and her purpose in life. I was glad to listen and ask questions, but I was puzzled by her angst. At the time, my purpose seemed so clear, I simply couldn't put myself in her shoes. Many years later, as I was asking myself what my own purpose in life was, I understood her anxieties and wished I could have offered her more when she had been struggling.

Some people who started out as friends became extended family. Alan and Tricia came into our lives in 1993 fresh out of college in Ohio. They were so enthusiastic after listening to the tape course that they traveled west intent on meeting us. Over the years of our ongoing relationship with them, we watched them try out our teachings on spirituality, money, relationships, and service, and embody them and in their own ways. Now they have each brought their own offerings to the world. They have been inspirations to me.

When Margaret read "The Possible Relationship," she became so excited by the concepts in it that she tracked us down. We were drawn in by her enthusiasm, spunk and commitment to community living. Over the many years of our relationship, Margaret followed her own star but brought us the calmness and clarity of age and experience.

Helen and Phil had written us about their experience of following the nine-step program after taking our financial seminar in Seattle. When Vicki and Joe were invited to appear on *CBS This Morning* after *Your Money or Your Life* was published, they reached out to this couple to see if they would be willing to be interviewed for the show about their experience doing the steps—and they said yes. Their enthusiasm was so genuine and heartfelt that we invited them over for dinner to get to know them better. The conversation was lively, not just about the financial program and how they were using it, but about our spiritual paths. Phil shared what a deep practice Vipassana meditation was for him. Helen said sheepishly that she didn't have a traditional spiritual practice—she just sat still, listened, and experienced joy—but her radiant face told me all I needed to know.

Guests

Hosting guests for dinner and the evening was an important focus for us. Some people seemed like kindred spirits; they brought inspiration and a sense of "these are our people." There was often an easy-going exchange of ideas and what was brewing in their personal or work lives or a sharing of life stories. What were they up to now? How were their projects and initiatives going? Where were their lives taking them? They often drew our truths out of us and reflected back to us what they were seeing and experiencing in us. Sometimes there was much laughter in the sheer delight at being with like-minded people, sharing our truths and stories, and hearing theirs. Even our serious discussions could be full of laughter. It was a pleasure to be with people who wanted to play the game of love and service. I learned so much from these encounters and found them stimulating.

I remember the thrill when Dr. Robert Muller, former assistant secretary-general of the United Nations, shared a meal with us. He was an eloquent speaker, and when he gave the blessing before eating, it moved me to tears. He asked God to help us to save this tiny, blue ball suspended in space and especially to help those of us around the table, and he expressed gratitude for life. He saw his area of expertise as making impossibilities into possibilities. He told us that our lifestyle, how we chose to live, was the fast track to sainthood, that lots of heat and pressure produce diamonds. I wrote in my diary later, "This is a good reminder to me when I'm not feeling up to the task." We drew incredible inspiration from guests like him.

We wanted to offer a space for guests to experience transformation or insight into their lives, and we gave a lot of thought to what might evoke such an experience. We felt that part of our mission was to challenge the status quo, which was Joe's specialty. Guests could choose to be curious and open or to react strongly and storm out the door (which happened more than once, literally and figuratively). We certainly could be passionate and intentional. With all ten of us present, a guest often described the experience as intense and intimidating, even though we did our best to be welcoming.

We were experts at drawing people out and listening. Some people left feeling heard and understood for the first time in their lives. Trivial conversation was tolerated up to a point, and then one of us would ask a probing question. Here are some examples:

- How *are* you? (Meaning, "How are you *really*?," not the short answer.)
- What is your life path? What do you want in life?
- What are you working on spiritually?
- What are your leading edges? (Meaning, "What is the focus of your internal growth right now?")
- What is love? What are the barriers to love?
- How do relationships work? How are your relationships— with your partner, parents, children?
- What draws you, motivates you? What moves you?
- Where are you in your life right now? (This was what the UV Family asked me back at Dinosaur National Monument).
- What do you want? What's pulling you?
- What's holding you back? How can we support you?

We tried to observe the following tenets in these conversations:

- Maintain focus and uplevel (i.e., move from superficial to deeper topics) at every opportunity, with the goal of deepening conversations with people.
- Be actively and creatively participating at every moment.

- If you were a listener, be alert to what might be missing.
- Be ready to catch the ball at any moment.
- Keep the ball in the air and steer it toward the net so that one of us (often Joe) could spike it. (Often the spiker got all the credit when his or her job wasn't any more or less important than anyone else's.)
- Find that balance between offering a challenging perspective or bringing up a hot-button topic and being sensitive to what a guest really wanted or where their limits were.

So we did what we did—and what created the transformation was in the other person. It was both the quality of our being and the content of the conversations that were important in creating a space for that. In some ways, we functioned as a mirror for our guests—they saw whatever they were meant to see, depending on their perspective, hang-ups, and proclivities. For one person, all it looked like was sex; for another, spirituality; for another, activism; for another, a cult; for another, love; and for another, a monastery. You had to have new eyes to see this new reality for what it was. Otherwise, we just looked like a weird group of people all living together.

We were constantly evaluating how we interacted with guests. For example, what worked and didn't work, when were our egos in the way, what did we perceive a particular guest might need—an experience of being loved and accepted for who they were, affirmation for the work they were doing in the world, inspiration for their next step in life?

When the ten of us would compare our impressions of a guest after they had left, we were often surprised that we each had a different perspective. One person would comment on how inspired they were by the guest's ideas. Another might have observed a vague or overt power struggle occurring with whomever this guest had perceived as having the most power. Still another of us would say, "I don't care what their faults are; I simply love them." It took self-awareness and courage to state a very different perspective from others, but every viewpoint would provide a more well-rounded picture of this person.

Chapter 7

What We Did: Our Work

Our work in the world through NRM was interwoven with and inseparable from our relationship and our foundation in Spirit. While the heartbeat was an outgrowth of who we were and how we related to one another, our work expressed this heartbeat and was an integral part of it. It was what made our group sing.

As the original four UV Family learned way back in Mexico, focusing on a vision and purpose larger than themselves and being of service to others were essential components to keeping the love and high spirits flowing and not getting bogged down in their needs, wants, and desires. Our overarching vision was to put more love out into the world and respond to the world's needs. We strove for unity among us at the level of our vision so we could be aligned and have maximum power and effectiveness. We promoted service as a route to personal health and well-being, as well as social revitalization. All our work came out of this desire to serve. We recognized that service was the natural impulse to care for what we recognized as being connected to us. This was love made manifest. It was this vision and the promise of meaningful work that were important draws for me when I met this crew at Dinosaur National Monument.

Our mission through NRM was to communicate another reality about how life could be lived (a new road map) and change the way people think about their lives. Our purpose was transformation of human consciousness, a radical shift in how we collectively under-stand our place in the universe and the purpose of human life. We were working together toward a "world that works for everyone" (a phrase we adopted from Werner Erhard). We used the metaphors of personal finances, health, and relationships to share our message of transfor-mation and personal empowerment since these were the three arenas where we had experience and expertise to share.

We continually asked ourselves, "How can we serve? What is the best use of our life energy? Where do our skills and passions meet with the world's needs? How can we be effective agents of social change?" We aligned our work with what we thought the world needed. We lis-tened to Spirit and waited for the *ring of rightness* (i.e., clarity based on a combination of logic and intuition) and group resonance.

All our work was imbued with a can-do spirit, thinking outside the box, humor, irreverence, integrity, excellence and picking a "big row to hoe" (another phrase Erhard often used). One of our favorite quotes was from the anthropologist Margaret Mead: "Never doubt that a small group of thoughtful, committed citizens can change the world: indeed, it's the only thing that ever has." We relied on this and used it to remind ourselves of our true power.

Joe and Vicki were our primary visionaries. They made intuitive leaps that led us to the right next step. But anyone who thought they had a clear bead on our vision would be heard out. When Joe or some-one else would begin painting a picture of what they saw that the world needed and what our piece in that could be, I would be exhila-rated. Expanding our views helped me see where I and we fit into the whole picture, what was possible, and what we were striving for.

Volunteerism was one of our core values, and we ran NRM as full-time volunteers. Most of us were already financially self-sufficient when we moved into the house, and within a few years, even the late-comers among us had enough income to live within their means. This meant that all ten of us could give our time without needing monetary compensation. We took our jobs no less seriously than any profes-sional, yet we had the opportunity to set our own hours, avoid burn out (most of the time), focus on our passions, experience a flow of creativity, innovate when systems didn't work, take on new responsibilities when we wanted to grow, and, generally, work at a sustainable level.

We each came to this endeavor with different skills and temperaments, so we each had our self-appointed roles. If someone had written job descriptions and advertised for people to fill them, they couldn't have found more perfect people to perform each role and offer their unique, specific contributions.

Vicki was a superb networker, speaker, and writer. She would sally forth into the world, happily engaging with other people and organizations, and come back with stories, insights, new perspectives, and creative ideas to share with the group.

Joe was keeper of the vision. Being a homebody whenever possible, he would stay tuned in to the news, watching the *Nightly Business Report*, reading *The Wall Street Journal* and the *Seattle Post-Intelligencer*, and keeping his finger on the pulse of the world, especially as it related to our work. He could sense trends, ways our message needed to be tweaked, or how we were veering off our main objectives. Often, he would be one step ahead of the rest of us, lighting the way.

Monica was the embodiment of our collective heart and offered compassionate listening and wisdom to the rest of us and anyone she was interacting with. She was our letter writer and handled both family- and work-related correspondence. Writing letters from the *we* perspective instead of the *I* required humility and a sense of the larger *us*. She was also our main editor, keeping our publications grammatically correct and on point with what we wanted to say. She was often our cheerleader, transmitting her enthusiasm and support for our work.

Evy thought through details and timelines for getting a job done. She was also a networker and inspiring speaker who brought many new ideas to the group. She was the visionary for and the primary communicator about our health work. And she was also one of our main cooks.

The rest of us were implementers of one kind or another, often working behind the scenes and occasionally stepping up to take a leadership role or do a public talk about some aspect of our work. Marcia was receptionist extraordinaire, fielding phone calls, conveying warmth and interest to whoever called, and often being the voice of NRM. In person, she had a welcoming presence, allowing others to feel seen by her and bringing out the best in those she interacted with. Over the years, she became something like an ambassador, volunteering at other organizations for months at a time. She would offer ideas from our work to other organizations and bring their ideas back to us.

One of Diane's natural roles was as a greeter, welcoming whomever came to our door and offering them tea. She was articulate and had an inner strength and self-assuredness. She also created and worked with our computer databases. Marilynn was one of our main cooks and also helped Joe with the daily filling of orders for our materials. She brought joy and gratitude to everything she did and to those around her.

Paula used her capacity for discernment and perspective to provide a unique point of view or way to hold some aspect of our work. You could rely on her to be thinking about our work in her own quiet way and offer much-needed clarity when the rest of us were so immersed in the details that we had lost perspective. She was director of our publications and also provided administrative support. Lynn did computer work—data entry, creating and managing databases, and desktop publishing our various materials. She brought passion to whatever she did. I applied my analytical brain to our various projects and helped with editing our written materials.

While we each had our roles in the family and in our work, we were each much more than that. And to some degree, we could become interchangeable parts. We certainly aspired to this—to be able to step in to fill a role if needed. We trained ourselves to be ready to catch the ball at any moment.

Once a year, we would gather for what we called an advance (why retreat when you can advance?) to gain a larger view on our work. The purpose of advances was to celebrate what we had accomplished, gain perspective, look for what we might be missing, course correct, ask where the leverage points were and brainstorm for our future work.

When we gathered in the living room on the day of an advance, the anticipation and excitement were palpable. We would have an easel with butcher paper and colored markers on it. Some of us would bring information we wanted to share with the group. The tape recorder would be running. And some of us would take notes. We would step back and remind ourselves of the purpose of NRM—the spirit of contribution. Then we would look at the past year's accomplishments and celebrate them.

Next we would ask the questions, "Given the state of the world, what is next? What is wanted and needed? What is being called for by the times we are living in and by Lola?" We called God Lola in reference to the song from *Damn Yankees*, "Whatever Lola Wants, Lola Gets." So listening to Lola was a prime directive. And somehow, it was easier to surrender to Lola than to God. We also asked, "What is our role? Where are the fulcrums, the leverage points?" There would be a sense of spaciousness, and the discussion would jump back and forth as we fed off one another. One year, someone called our process "Lola-centric participatory anarchy." It was usually an enlivening experience.

We often ended up with a to-do list for the coming year that seemed to me impossible to get done. Some years, I would say to myself, "My God! What have we done?!" But we usually accomplished the main items on our list. Throughout the year, we would hearken back to these goals and evaluate where we were; the effectiveness of our talks, educational materials, and events; and what needed to be done next—or what was misguided or needed adjusting. This would keep us on track throughout the year.

Our Money and Sustainability Work

The financial work started out as a means to free people up to be of service by helping them achieve some level of financial independence. The nine-step program was based on awareness, fulfillment, and choice, not on budgeting or deprivation. A key to the program was an honest evaluation of whether an expenditure actually brought the person satisfaction, was aligned with their life purpose, and supported the kind of world they wanted to live in. Simplifying their lives and discovering how much money was enough for them—not too little, but not excess—by following the program's steps resulted in a lower-consumption, higher-fulfillment lifestyle. This allowed many people to step away from the nine-to-five rat race and "making a dying." Others who didn't become financially independent still found that following the steps freed them up to experience more happiness, freedom, and meaning in their lives.

At the time, high-interest, 30-year US Treasury bonds were the investment of choice because they met the criteria of safety, liquidity, and high yield. Today, the low interest rates on these bonds makes them a poor choice for investing. The 2018 edition of *Your Money or Your Life* offers other suggestions for investment that are more realistic for the current times. And folks continue to find that they can free up a lot of life energy for the causes they love by following the steps.

When Marilynn first heard Joe give his seminar on the nine-step program, she knew immediately, "I can do this." She went through the course step by step, working as a cook and caterer, until she achieved financial independence six years later. In reflecting on that experience, she says, "It was revolutionary, really." And to this day, she readily shares this experience with others.

By the time we were living in the house, the all-day financial seminars drew four hundred people at a whack, and it took all of us to host them. Soon we produced the cassette tape course *Transforming Your Relationship with Money and Achieving Financial Independence* that we had started working on in Jenner. Now Joe, who had the hardest job of being the presenter, and the rest of us wouldn't have to continue doing the seminars, and we could reach a much larger audience. Thousands of tape courses would go out our doors in the years before *Your Money or Your Life* was published in 1992, and even after.

A pivotal moment came in 1989 when we heard about the Globescope Pacific Assembly conference in Los Angeles. Its purpose was to report on the Brundtland Commission's findings that there was a link between economic development and worldwide environmental degradation and resource depletion. The report concluded that governments and business leaders needed to promote sustainable development, defined as "development that meets the needs of the present without compromising the ability of future generations to meet their own needs."

Evy felt a strong internal directive that this was on our plate, and she convinced Vicki to attend. This marked a turning point for Vicki and our group. At the conference, speaker after speaker said that consumption in North America was the biggest barrier to sustainable development. But they all shrugged as if to say that there was no way to address this. Vicki thought to herself, "We have the solution! We have the way out of overconsumption! Our financial program teaches people how to consume less of the planet's finite resources by looking carefully at how they spend money and why, and what expenses are truly fulfilling. This process helps you define what is enough, thus reducing overconsumption."

At the conference, Noel Brown, a senior environmental official at the United Nations, said that the world had a ten-year window of opportunity to reverse global warming before it was beyond human ability to alter. Vicki returned from that conference with such passion and conviction that she set us all on a larger trajectory. We felt that the 1990s was our decade to do our part to turn things around, and this galvanized us to give it our all. We began to see that our teachings were strategies not only for *individual* change but also for *social* change. We committed ourselves to the task of educating and empowering individuals to be conscious creators of their own future and the future of our world.

We took to heart the admonition by Dr. Robert Muller when he was our dinner guest that "the single most important contribution any of us can make to the planet is a return to frugality." We tried to live this in our personal lives, and we promoted it through our financial work. So our frugality mission took on a larger scope at this point: to save the world by changing the way people think about money and by reducing overconsumption. More and more of our work was focused on creating a sustainable world before environmental degradation, resource depletion, climate change, and species loss became irreversible.

Vicki described this shift as follows: "The dominant story of our time is 'more is always better.' We hope to help cleanse our collective vision so we may learn to live within the Earth's material limits while learning to soar as we deepen our relationship with the wonder of life. Therefore, we are working at the level of cultural transformation, the story we live as a people."

Throughout our years together, we used the term *saving the world*. Much later in our lives, we realized this concept was fraught with problems. For example, the earth may not be what needs saving—it may be the human population and the habitats and resources we need to support our existence that need saving. And at a deeper level, perhaps this ideal led to burnout for some of us. But for most of our time together, this term was used to describe the larger vision of creating a sustainable world, a world we wanted to live in. Yes, we might have been chasing rainbows, but we liked that challenge, and just maybe, we could move the world toward sustainability.

In addition to being a leader in the frugality movement, our work now expanded to include writing our inaugural annual newsletter, *FI News & Notes*, for our mailing list of people who had attended the financial seminar or done the tape course. FI stands for financial intelligence, financial integrity, and financial independence. We called people who applied FI thinking through doing the nine-step program Flers. In addition, we helped edit an issue of *In Context* magazine on "What Is Enough," focusing on how to bring our lives into alignment with what the Earth can sustain and what gives us fulfillment. Also, Vicki began participating in the US Citizens Network on the United Nations Conference on Environment and Development. This network of nongovernmental organizations shared its views on sustainable development with the US government in preparation for the first Earth Summit in Rio de Janeiro, Brazil, in 1992. Later, Vicki served on the Population and Consumption Task Force of the President's Council on Sustainable Development, established by President Bill Clinton.

Most importantly, we realized that although the tape course was reaching a nationwide audience, a book would reach even more people. So Vicki, Joe, and Monica picked up the book that they had started back in Jenner, reenvisioned it, and decided it was time to write what would become *Your Money or Your Life*.

Your Money or Your Life

From the very beginning, the making of *Your Money or Your Life* was a group process. We huddled up in early 1991, and after everyone weighed in on it, we made a group decision to proceed with the book. We knew the possible implications—that it would be our primary focus for the next year or more and we'd be committed to publicizing it. In short, it would change our lives—and it did. Because each of us was part of the decision, we all *owned* the book and the process of writing it.

Writing began in earnest once Viking Penguin became our publisher, and the great, eight-month book boogie (that is, a priority project we undertook as an all-out push with intense focus, determination, and speed) began. Over time, each of us found our niche in writing what we called the *FI Book*, and our synergy was at its finest. It was like we were playing a symphony that year. Joe was the conductor in his role as visionary and overviewer. He also played the sax, composing the melody for the prologue, last chapter, and epilogue, and creating the riff for the warning to readers. Vicki was first violin. She was our main wordsmith, writing most of the chapters, weaving and soaring and connecting. Monica played the bass, keeping the (heart)beat steady throughout the writing process. She also played second violin, trimming unnecessary notes from the score with her editing skills.

The rest of us would come in on cue for solo work. Although Evy and I were immersed in the ALS Project at the time, we also joined the orchestra. Evy brought in a rich cello at just the right time to accompany Vicki on her violin, as we will see. And I played an occasional solo oboe by being a writing muse for Joe and making sure the movements in the symphony were in the correct order and that the music flowed. Lynn was our pianist (and a real-life pianist), doing some of the necessary computer work. Diane on the tuba did the strenuous work of compiling articles on frugality and money in a database. Marilynn on the piccolo checked all the footnotes and some of the facts we quoted in the book. And Paula on the bassoon did editing and proofreading. Our clarinetist, Marcia, was the receptionist, keeping NRM running while others were occupied with the book.

When a chapter draft would be ready, all of us would read it. Then we would gather and tune up for the feedback session, praising or critiquing as warranted. The one we all remember the best was Chapter 4. Many of us were trying to find a kind way of saying that we couldn't follow Vicki's melody, that the chapter just didn't work, but Joe just blurted out, "We all fell asleep!" The first violinist responded gracefully and gallantly went back to practicing her violin. It takes a big person to take that kind of blunt feedback and respond without defensiveness. Evy on the cello came to her aid, and they produced a revised version of the chapter that really worked.

It was a great experience, and we all ended up feeling like authors even though only Joe and Vicki would appear on the cover. Here's what I wrote in my diary back then: "As a team, we reached a new level of synergy higher than we've ever achieved before and with more people involved. Everyone seemed to call forth their best and be willing and able to go to new individual heights (levels of competence, not letting our egos get in the way, and working well with others). This was true for me as well, although I 'crashed' immediately afterward."

Joe reminded us that boogies were sprints, while the long haul was a marathon. After a sprint, you need to rest. If you're doing a boogie amid a marathon, you may not be able to recuperate sufficiently without more personal maintenance. This seems to have been the case with me, and it took some time to recover my energy.

Early on in conversations among ourselves and with Viking Penguin, it became apparent that if we wanted this book to have maximum visibility and impact, we should aim for it to be on the *New York Times* Best Sellers list. This idea fit right in with our modus operandi of dreaming big and picking a large row to hoe. Vicki collaborated intensively with the team at Viking Penguin to create an effective marketing campaign to publicize the book. Joe was willing to do major interviews, while Vicki was willing to speak anywhere at any venue—whatever it took.

The two of them appeared on *CBS This Morning* soon after the book was out, followed by *The Oprah Winfrey Show*. Vicki was on *Oprah* again a year or two later. Her speaking tour was daunting, with radio and TV interviews, book signings, talks, and magazine and newspaper interviews. Finally, when she found herself at a tiny radio station in the middle of what seemed like a cow pasture, she reached the limits of what she would do for the cause.

Between all the publicity and our mailings to our network of FIers, there were enough book sales to achieve our goal of putting *Your Money or Your Life* on the *New York Times* Best Sellers list. It was also on the *BusinessWeek* Best-Seller List for five years and was referred to as the bible of the frugality movement.

Today, over 785,000 books have been sold, and it has been translated into many languages. In 2018, Vicki adapted the information and steps for the current times and specifically for millennials, and a new edition was published. So even today, more than twenty-five years after the first edition was published, it is a go-to book for many millennials who were kids back then, or not even born.

We realized that part of why the book was so popular in the 1990s was its blend of pragmatism and romanticism. It wasn't ideological, so it appealed to conservatives and liberals alike. And the timing was right, with many people feeling enslaved by their work and their debt, and wanting more meaning in their lives than their jobs provided.

We developed other supporting materials including a study guide to use with *Your Money or Your Life* for groups working with the nine-step program, a couple of pamphlets (one detailing the problem of over-consumption and the other a lifestyle self-assessment questionnaire), a position paper on overconsumption, and a League of Women Voters white paper (an educational guide) titled "From 'Excess' to 'Enough': Shifting the Culture of Consumption." We realized there were hundreds of avid FIers whose lives had changed from doing the program. They were anxious to share their experience and wisdom with others, so we formed a speaker's bureau to organize them and offer guidance and ideas on how to communicate the FI message. Eventually there would be a workplace outreach program to bring these ideas into the workplace.

The Affluenza Story

In our work to reduce overconsumption, as with all our work, our projects were chosen based on a combination of tuning in to Lola (remember, our term for God), dreaming big, paying attention to synchronicities and intuition, and recognizing opportunities that presented themselves. The story about the making of John de Graaf and Vivia Boe's PBS documentary film, *Affluenza*, was a perfect example of this. I wasn't directly involved, but I just marvel at how each step led to the next one. This film looked at how society's overconsumption and materialism eat away at our personal lives and families, erode our communities, and damage our environment, using the term *affluenza* to describe this state. It also highlights people working toward a more sustainable way of life.

According to John, "We did not invent the word 'affluenza' . . . but my coproducer, coauthors, and I certainly popularized the term. We defined it as 'a painful, contagious, socially transmitted condition of overload, debt, anxiety, and waste resulting from the dogged pursuit of more.'"[1]

It came about in the following way. Vicki was invited to a conference the US Citizens Network on the United Nations Conference on Environment and Development was hosting for its members. Before the conference, she challenged the network chairman to reserve accommodations that were consistent with his talk about sustainability instead of the lavish lodgings he had chosen. When he refused, she wrote a letter to him and the US Department of State pointing out this glaring discrepancy.

Around this time, we had been envisioning a documentary on overconsumption. When Vicki attended an Environmental Grantmakers Association meeting, she made a strong case for funding media related to environmental issues. A woman named Susan from PEW Charitable Trusts came to that meeting via train, having heard about and been influenced by Vicki's letter to the network chairman. She and Vicki struck up a friendship. After the meeting, while Vicki was still on the

---

[1] John de Graff, "Co-Author of *Affluenza*: 'I'm Appalled by the Ethan Couch Decision,'" *TIME*, Dec. 14, 2013, https://ideas.time.com/2013/12/14/co-author-of-affluenza-im-appalled-by-the-ethan-couch-decision/.

East Coast, Susan reached out to us in Seattle via letter. Joe had a strong intuition that Vicki should see Susan while she was still back east if at all possible, so Vicki arranged to meet with her. At that time, Susan and a colleague were in the middle of writing a grant proposal to their board for money for environmental projects. As Vicki painted a picture of a documentary on overconsumption, Susan turned to her colleague and said, "Let's write money for that into our grant proposal."

Meanwhile, back in Seattle, John de Graaf, who was a well-respected filmmaker, left a message out of the blue for Vicki to call him when she returned. When Vicki and Evy met with John, they found out that he had just finished a project and didn't know what he would be doing next. NRM offered to fund the treatment for a documentary on overconsumption if he would produce it. When Susan saw the treatment, she convinced the PEW board to fund it.

People arrived on John's doorstep who wanted to volunteer their time for this project, and John and his crew invited our participation in designing the film. Joe pointed out that reducing consumption was a bridge issue, crossing all lines of politics and religion, and John incorporated that into his own thinking. Somewhere along the line, Vicki came up with the term affluenza on a plane flight. When she mentioned it to John, it stuck. (Later, we discovered that the term had first been coined by someone else who had written a book by that title.)

Evy spent many hours making logs of each interview tape. Vicki and Evy helped shape the film, with input from all of us, devoting many hours per week to the project and suggesting many of the people who ended up being interviewed for the film. But they stayed enough out of the way to let John's brilliance come through on the film.

When we discovered that there was no money for publicity for the film, we donated $25,000 for that. The team at KCTS-TV, a PBS member television station in Seattle, did an excellent job of using that money to publicize *Affluenza*, which aired in 1997. The response was overwhelming. Ninety calls came in to the New York City PBS office, all positive. That was unheard of by KCTS. In 2001, the book *Affluenza* was published, based on this film, and it became a bestseller. Now affluenza is almost a household word, and it has even been used as an excuse for bad behavior. You might recall the teen who killed four people while driving drunk in 2013, and his defense was affluenza—that he grew up too rich to know right from wrong.

Marauds

Some of the braver and zanier people in our group (not me!) loved to think up marauds—doing something crazy but effective to wake people up.

We loved Buy Nothing Day, an initiative started by the Canadian magazine *Adbusters* to buy nothing on the day after Thanksgiving, traditionally the biggest shopping day of the year in the United States and known as Black Friday. To celebrate that day, some of our group would go down to Westlake Park in Seattle, across from the Westlake Shopping Center, to stage an observance. One time, they made a medical booth out of cardboard with a sign saying, HAVE AFFLUENZA? THE DOCTOR IS IN. Monica, dressed in a white lab coat with a clown's red nose, played doctor. The cure for affluenza? Cutting up your credit cards. There were samples of cut-up credit cards, and scissors (and encouragement) were offered for anyone wanting to do that. Others walked around singing "Down at the Shopping Mall."

"Down at the Shopping Mall"
(Words by Monica, sung to "Down by the Riverside")

> *I'm gonna cut up my credit cards*
> *Down at the shopping mall*
> *Down at the shopping mall*
> *Down at the shopping mall*
> *Gonna cut up my credit cards*
> *Down at the shopping mall*
> *And run up debt no more.*
>
> *I ain't gonna run up debt no more*
> *I ain't gonna run up debt no more*
> *I ain't gonna blow it at the store*

I ain't gonna run up debt no more
I ain't gonna run up debt no more
I ain't buying in to wanting More.

Another such adventure was the Valentine's Day maraud. Vicki was returning from a trip, and Monica and a friend, Margaret, picked her up at the airport. They were sporting large, heart-shaped signs on their backs and fronts suggesting ways to express love and affection that didn't involve spending a lot of money. They read, MONEY CAN'T BUY ME LOVE; FREE LOVE—A HUG, A KISS, PRAISE; GIVE GIFTS FROM THE HEART, NOT THE PURSE; GIVE KISSES INSTEAD OF TRINKETS; and MAKE LOVE, NOT DEBT—GIVE LOVE, NOT STUFF.

From there, they went to Northgate Mall in Seattle. The three of them, all dressed in red and adorned with these signs, walked up and down inside the mall, even offering free hugs when appropriate. They were ultimately asked to leave by several security guards with no sense of humor.

They would return from these events enthusiastic, enlivened, and happy. I was too timid to join in, but I sure appreciated the spirit and loved hearing about their antics.

Our Health Work and the ALS Project

From the day Evy got out of her wheelchair and walked down the sidewalk, she was passionate about sharing her transformative experience of healing with other people, especially medical professionals. She wrote essays and articles, and gave talks and workshops. She described the steps to her healing and how important it was that the medical community broaden its perspective on the connection among mind, body, and spirit in illness and healing. She envisioned transforming the practice of Western medicine through doctors who could be agents of change by integrating psycho-social aspects of a patient's life into their treatment plan.

The seeds for the ALS Project were planted in the desert in 1985 where the four UV Family members that I first met were taking a retreat (no, make that an advance!) to "listen" for what they should be focusing on next. Evy was particularly interested in doing a project that would document the mind-body connection in disease in a way that could convince the medical community. She realized ALS was a perfect disease to study because there was no known cause and no known treatment or cure to obscure the results. She thought, "Wouldn't it be great to do a medical research project on the mind-body connection in ALS?" They let the idea simmer.

Soon after, she was invited to speak at a conference on ALS in Italy because she had survived this disease. Scientists who were studying ALS would be gathered from around the world. It was there that Evy first met Sue Wiedenfeld, a clinical psychologist, and Al Hillel, an ENT physician specializing in swallowing disorders, both from Seattle. They all decided this idea of a study was great, and the ALS Project was born. They envisioned publishing a paper in a major peer-reviewed medical journal. Evy brought the idea back home and got the enthusiastic go-ahead from the rest of us. From then on, among ourselves, we called this paper that we would get published our *blockbuster paper*, again reaching for the stars.

The original questions the study posed were:

- Does the ALS patient have a psycho-social profile that is different from the normal population?
- Is there a psycho-social profile of spouses and caregivers of ALS patients?
- If so, is it predictable by the patient's psycho-social profile or disease state?
- Can the rate of disease progression in ALS be predicted by any psycho-social variable?

They designed the study to measure psychological, spiritual, and physical well-being in ALS patients in three metropolitan areas (Seattle, San Francisco, and Philadelphia). Tests were given to 143 patients and 123 of their spouses or caregivers seven times during an eighteen-month period. They used a combination of normed and validated psychological tests, such as the Beck Depression Inventory, plus a physical assessment questionnaire designed by Al and his ENT team, and a long questionnaire designed by Evy, Sue, and Al.

Consistent with our principles of volunteerism and service, we decided that this project would be based on dedication and commitment rather than on money raised through grants. Thus we consciously chose to not seek funding. Our inspiration was Dr. Carlton Gadjusek, who won the Nobel Prize in the physiology/medicine category. He was asked to address the question, "If the ALS research community had $5 million in 5 years, what could they do, how far would they get?" Outspokenly, he said they wouldn't get very far because it wasn't about money but dedication. Eradication of smallpox and kuru (a fatal disease of the nervous system that Gadjusek studied) happened because of dedication, not because of large budgets and huge research centers.

NRM covered all incidental expenses for the years of the study, totaling $15,000 (for postage, phone calls, photocopying, computers, and travel), compared with the $350,000 that this kind of project would normally have cost for a five-year study in the late 1980s.

Sue and Al were already willing to co-lead the study with Evy on a volunteer basis. Top-ranking computer consultants and statisticians looking for ways to contribute saw that this project fit with their heartfelt desires. As one physician said, "I am doing three other research projects that are funded, and yet for some reason, this study is the one I find most satisfying and gives me the greatest sense of contributing to life."

There ended up being fifty volunteers who worked on the study. The tests and questionnaires had to be copied, and packets had to be prepared for each patient and spouse for all seven rounds of testing. We affectionately called the assembly of these packets "collation therapy." Someone had to schedule every appointment, do follow-up phone calls, and send out questionnaires that could be filled out ahead of time. Travel itineraries to the two West Coast study sites had to be organized, coordinating with the volunteers who were trained to administer the tests and assessments at home visits. Monica, who had some nursing training, coordinated this data collection phase and conducted a lot of the home visits. I occasionally accompanied her, while others in our group either assisted her or were primary testers. A nurse in Philadelphia volunteered to test patients there, and Evy and I visited several times to support her and provide continuity between the sites.

We were asking very personal, profound questions. Many patients and their caregivers were simply struggling to adjust to the rapid loss of function so common in this disease and were doing their best just to get through each day. Sometimes we were amazed when one of the severely disabled patients would answer the question, "How do you feel about your life?" with "I have a lot to live for." Many of us had the experience that some patients who had had the disease the longest and had the most severe cases shone with what seemed like an inner light. They seemed guileless, and it was a privilege to be in their presence. It was unexpected and provided food for thought. We asked ourselves, "What is happening for these people who have come into this place of innocence in the face of not being able to eat, talk, walk, move, or breathe on their own—any of the functions we think of as necessary for quality of life?" There was an almost childlike quality, no personal issues in the way, almost as if they were moving into another realm. One spouse, reflecting on her ill husband, said, "The patient has to give up being a *doing* and just become a *being*." An amazing, unblocked love sometimes flowed through them, and you found yourself looking into the eyes of unconditional love. In addition, some people had a marvelous sense of humor and, because we didn't expect that, it was that much more welcome.

I was moved by my experience of being with the patients and their spouses. Here we were supposed to be dispassionate scientists, but at the same time, we were being changed in our very beings by the experience. I started having dreams such as this one about being with someone with ALS who was dying:

> *I am holding a dying man whom I don't know, but I am crying in grief for him. Suddenly a shift happens, and I experience an inner sense of peace and perceive that we are in a space of light together, the space*

of love. I look up at him, no longer crying but smiling and knowing it is
okay for him to die. We are at that moment "in love" together.

By the time we were done with patient testing, we had made 735 visits to patients and their families, asking 346,856 questions, all of which had to be processed and entered in the computer. First the standard psychological tests had to be scored, the answers on the questionnaires had to be coded, and everything that would be recorded in the computer had to be marked with a green highlighter. (We called this process "greening," and it was laborious.) A data dictionary defining each variable in the database had to be created and then all the data entered in the database. Accuracy was essential each step of the way.

All of us had some role in the ALS study, especially in the years before *Your Money or Your Life* was being written. Marilynn coordinated the Seattle volunteers who helped process the tests and questionnaires, and Paula often joined in with the other volunteers. Joe and Evy learned RBase, a database program, and created a computer database for all the data. Lynn created the data dictionary and did data entry.

Then there was the extensive statistical analysis and writing of papers. Evy and I had ongoing meetings with Al and Sue where we discussed the focus of our analyses and the content of the papers. Evy and I became the hands-on statistical analysis team, both of us learning what we needed to know about statistical analysis and what computer programs we needed to use. This data analysis phase overlapped with the book boogie, so our house was jumping with activity.

We were blessed with substantial guidance from statisticians at the University of California, Los Angeles and the University of Washington. When Evy and I had, to our dismay, filled fifty three-inch binders with statistical printouts, a wonderful professor of statistics at the University of Washington took us under wing, offering us perspective on our progress and advice about how to proceed. He reassured us, saying, "This is just the kill-a-tree phase of analysis." We were in awe of our good fortune to be able to consult with him.

Evy and I had totally different personalities. For example, she would get excited about possibilities, while my excitement would build gradually as the evidence came in. Sometimes I would experience her enthusiasm as unrealistic, and sometimes she would accuse me of being a wet blanket. We could both be opinionated and think our way was the right way. But we needed each other's perspectives, and out of that, we'd ultimately come up with the best way. One time, Evy and I erupted at each other, but we immediately saw how ridiculous that was. We both admitted we had already been feeling tense before our meeting and burst out laughing.

We worked hard, but we found ways to have fun at the same time. One year, the hottest day of the summer found Evy and me in her office with the curtains drawn, sitting at our card table under the ceiling fan stark naked, doing our work. Of course we had to make lemonade out of this lemon day, so we memorialized the event with a photo. After we lightened up about how hot we were, we got busy with our work.

At some point, Joe got impatient with the official statistical analysis Evy and I were doing. He asked, "This is all well and good, but do we have any results worth talking about?" He created what he called a play database where he could do his own version of unofficial data analysis. In his usual way of finding easy solutions to complex problems, he would sort the patients, say, from the least to the most hopeless (based on their Beck Hopelessness Scale scores) and look to see if there had been more deaths of the most hopeless than the least. And indeed, that is what he found. Although this simple approach didn't account for severity of illness, length of disease, or age, he convinced himself and us that it was worth continuing our meticulous and rigorous analysis.

Evy and I would take Joe's play data and try to understand what they showed. We made diagrams and taped them to the walls of Evy's office to try to tease apart what this mind-body connection looked like. During this time, Evy had a dream in which the various aspects we were studying (e.g., physical, mental, emotional, spiritual, and social) were laid out and how the data might fit. She woke up and excitedly drew what she had seen in the dream. That diagram became a touchstone for our thinking and organizing of the data.

Finally, the main data analysis was done. It showed that a person with psychological distress had a risk of dying during the study that was 6.8 times higher than those with psychological well-being, after adjusting for confounding variables like age, length of illness, and severity of disease.

Now it was time to actually write this blockbuster paper we'd been envisioning for so long. This was a painstaking process of trying to communicate the results as succinctly as we could, and it was laborious. Evy and I would write a draft, read it with a critical eye, and get feedback from Al and Sue. When Evy or I would react to the other's concerns about the latest draft, we would step back and remind ourselves of our common goal of writing the finest paper we could—and we knew we needed each other. Then we'd get back to work on yet another draft.

At one point, I wrote this in my diary:

It's been two years that we've been writing the paper and at least nine months that we've been writing and rewriting the paper for actual submission. Each rethinking makes it a better paper, but I'm nearing the end of what I'm willing to do. It's like climbing a mountain and reaching one false summit after another.

After twenty-nine drafts and a stack of printed rewrites measuring a foot high, our paper was accepted for publication. All our work was distilled down to seven pages in the journal *Archives of Neurology* (now called *JAMA Neurology*).[2] We'd achieved our goal of writing a scientific paper for a peer-reviewed medical journal documenting the mind-body connection in ALS, a disease that wasn't thought to have such a connection. While it wasn't the blockbuster of our dreams, it was one more study challenging Western medicine's approach to illness.

Collaborating with Sue and Al, we wrote several more scientific papers on various aspects of the project, as well as a patient report on what we learned from the whole study. The latter was written in

---

[2]E.R. McDonald, S.A. Wiedenfeld, A. Hillel, C.L. Carpenter, R.A. Walter. 1994. "Survival in Amyotrophic Lateral Sclerosis: The Role of Psychological Factors." *Archives of Neurology*, 51 (January): 17-23.

layman's terms for patients, families, and caregivers to help them cope with the realities of ALS. Over the course of the project, Evy gave forty-eight talks in five countries, reporting on various aspects of the study to organizations such as the American Holistic Medical Association, the National Wellness Conference, the Biofeedback Conference, the Society of Behavioral Medicine, the Barrows Neurological Institute, the American Association of Neuroscience Nurses, and the Motor Neurone Disease Association in England.

By this time, Evy's and my interest in pursuing more analysis of our data was waning, but we realized there was a wealth of information yet to be gleaned from it. We wanted to give the database to someone who could use it. About this time, a researcher at the University of Kentucky contacted us, hoping to borrow some of our data for a particular aspect of ALS that he was exploring. When we broached the idea of him being caretaker of the whole database, he was interested and could imagine graduate students using this data set. We were excited about his interest and vowed to make this happen. Getting the database ready to be turned over to someone else turned out to be an arduous process involving a final check of the data for accuracy and documenting every variable that would take me ten more years to complete.

Vicki had what was, for me, a startling perspective as she observed our process with the ALS Project:

> At some point in the ALS project, Evy said, "I'm quitting." I remember thinking, "That's cool." We've got to be able to quit what we're doing at any moment. You can pick the job up at any moment, but if you can't say, "I'm fed up. That's how I am right now. If I don't see one more statistic, I will be fine," then you're trapped. Then you can choose to pick the job up again, but if you can't choose to set it down, you're trapped. Trapped will produce stress. And that doesn't mean to be irresponsible or not to keep our commitments. You can say, "I don't feel like doing this; I'm terrified doing this," and then do it, but don't lie about how you feel about doing it or lay it onto other people or projects that others have expectations. There's something very basic about that, which seems key to me.

Well, Evy did quit later on, but I never learned this lesson. I never was able to say, "I quit," until a decade later when I finally completed the tedious and painstaking work on the database so I could hand it over to the University of Kentucky.

Our Relationship Work

While our financial and health work were overt, our relationship work was more subtle. In the earlier days of the UV Family, they gave talks on their relationship and group marriage, and were up front about it. And we had written "The Possible Relationship" describing the principles—such as having a purpose larger than the relationship—that made our marriage work. But we found that readers often misconstrued what we were saying, interpreting everything through a sexual lens or wanting to pattern their own relationships or community after ours instead of taking the concepts and creating their own form. These were unintended consequences that made us leery of sharing this more widely.

Also, since we wanted to appear respectable to mainstream America for our financial work and the ALS Project, we did not emphasize or tout this article or our relationship except when someone expressed a genuine interest. We hoped that how we operated in our daily lives and out in the world reflected the quality of our relationship. We certainly made ourselves available to individuals who entered our lives and were exploring relationships or had relationship issues. We spent countless hours listening to them, offering our perspectives and sharing insights from our own experience.

Our Philanthropy

As a charitable organization, NRM awarded nearly eight hundred separate grants totaling almost $1 million to many nonprofits. Most grants ranged from $500 to $3,000 and were made to grassroots organizations with low overhead where most of the grant would directly support their work instead of salaries. We liked to give a boost to fledgling organizations that were addressing an important aspect of creating a sustainable world. We preferred to fund organizations that were working on root causes rather than providing Band-Aids. However, we did have a local action program, funded by my mother, to help the homeless in Seattle. One year when my folks were visiting us, their motor home broke down, and my mother was so distressed that she told God that if she got home safely, she'd donate a portion of her pension every year to support the homeless. Well, she got home safely and kept her promise. It felt good to offer tangible help to our local community, and we found many organizations with mostly volunteer staff where a little bit of money could go a long way.

Chapter 8

Operating the Well-Oiled Machine

Vicki says of our group:

We sometimes called ourselves a well-oiled machine—and it took a well-oiled machine to bring Your Money or Your Life, this understanding, out into the world, to create that ice-breaker boat that would go through the solid ice of the culture and break it up in big chunks. It took the power of the total focus of this whole group of people to do this work. And we loved doing it.

Our well-oiled machine resulted from the interplay of three fundamental aspects:

- Individual spiritual base and growth, *drawing us deep into ourselves*, enabling us to bring forth our very best. Each of us had to have internal motivation and commitment.
- Intimacy *drawing us together*, creating closeness and solidity among us.
- Higher purpose *drawing us outward*, allowing group synergy to happen and a sense of being able to make a real difference.

Any outward success gave us positive feedback, although we

always reminded ourselves not to count on seeing results as our reason for doing what we did.

We were a high-performance, synergistic team. We were tightly woven, with strong bonds among us, aligned at all levels. We had a common mission and purpose. We always had a goal and a plan. And sometimes it was an outrageous goal that seemed almost impossible, like reducing overconsumption in North America. At our best, we *were* this well-oiled machine—like a rowing crew, synchronized and synergistic, becoming an organism. At our worst, it felt like we were slaves, laboring to row this heavy galley. During our whole time together, we had the opportunity many times a day to experience one or the other: to hold the highest possible expression or sink to the lowest. Luckily, we weren't all low at the same time and someone would invariably inspire those of us who were low to reframe or shift to a higher state of consciousness. We were a work in progress, individually and collectively.

We also paid attention to whether we appeared to be going with or against the flow of the universe. Roadblocks were a sign that we might be going against the flow, and it was time to reassess our direction. Our group cohesion allowed us to be flexible and change our mind without negative consequences among us because we were all listening for Lola, and the change would resonate for everyone at least to some degree.

There were many aspects that kept the well-oiled machine humming and were also part of the underpinning of the heartbeat: our personality and style, how we chose our work, our purpose and intention, our decision-making and leadership strategies, clear communication and coordination, looking out for the whole, power and empowerment, cocreation, collaboration with others, and celebration and recognition.

Our Personality and Style

Our group had a particular personality, style, and way of doing things. Any one of us might not have embodied all these qualities and attitudes (I certainly didn't), but overall, you could count on the group to have them.

We had self-confidence and felt free to express our beliefs and be true to ourselves. We had a "you can count on me" attitude. There was a spirit of curiosity, enthusiasm, optimism, and loving engagement with life. We were on a Grand Adventure together, and our intention was to leave the world a better place through our work. We aimed to "keep our knees loose and our glove well oiled." This baseball phrase meant being flexible and ready to move in any direction, turn on a dime and catch anything life threw our way.

A sense of the absurd and being outrageous were qualities always close at hand. We had fun. Some might have called us subversive because although we were outrageous, we also acted under the radar where people seldom detected that we were behaving out of the ordinary. As I mentioned earlier, "Make hamburger out of all sacred cows, especially our own," was one of our mottos. We took ourselves and our devotion very seriously—and not seriously at all. If we couldn't laugh at what we held sacred, we risked locking ourselves into ideology and righteousness.

We aimed to be free from encumbering concepts, practices, and possessions. Individually and collectively, we practiced the frugality that we preached. We had each found our point of enoughness and stewarded our income wisely so our time was freed up for our work. And we ran the household simply and frugally.

Strategies for Choosing Our Work

We tried to get as close as possible to the source of a problem, to root cause. We always looked for the *trim tab*, like the tiny device on the rudder of an ocean liner that, with a small adjustment, allowed the rudder to turn the ship. We found places where a small effort, strategically applied, could make a big difference. We aimed to think outside the box, to stay with contradictions, complexity, and entrenched viewpoints until a new perception emerged. We thought in terms of possibility rather than limitation. We said yes to God-size tasks and going beyond our known limits because we believed that life begins when you're in over your head. Our approach was radical, turning ideas onto their heads to see them from a new angle. We were willing to risk on behalf of our ideals. And we tried to keep it simple, doing the essential and accomplishing what seemed most important.

Purpose and Intention

George Bernard Shaw said, "This is the true joy in life, the being used for a purpose *recognized by yourself as a mighty one.*" This saying was a touchstone for us. Our mighty purpose could be described as making a positive difference or putting love out into the world. And one of the byproducts of living our purpose was the joy that Shaw talked about.

When I met the UV Family at Dinosaur National Monument, I had given up on making a difference in the world. But it didn't take me long to see and learn and experience the ways they were making a difference both in the world and in other people's lives. And I desperately wanted my life to count for something and make a positive impact on the world. Living and working alongside other passionate people with the same desire was beyond my wildest dreams. I never lost sight of our jointly held purpose or my gratitude to be doing meaningful work connected to realizing this purpose.

Our group generated strong intentions to fulfill our purpose and reach our goals. We knew from Peter M. Senge's *The Fifth Discipline: The Art & Practice of the Learning Organization* that the creative tension between a strong vision or intention and one's current reality would promote movement toward one's goal. We were focused, efficient, and no-nonsense. We needed everyone's energy focused on our joint projects, our mutually shared dream. One of our mottos was, "Know what you are doing and why," a phrase adopted from Robert S. de Ropp's *The Master Game: Beyond the Drug Experience.* That alone is a worthy spiritual practice! And we tried to live our daily lives with that kind of intention.

Tasting, seeing, and feeling what it would be like to live my ideals pulled me ever so slowly toward them. It didn't matter that they sometimes seemed elusive —something you move toward but never reach—because they kept me alert to what was in the way of living them and they kept me on course. Living with others who had similar ideals kept those ideals front and center, and allowed me to be supported and spurred on by others.

Of course, there's a difference between being *intentional* and being *driven*, and I could slip into the latter if I wasn't careful. Intention has more space around it—it comes from the ground of your being—while being driven resides more in the ego and is more future-driven.

We also had a motto for keeping our priorities straight: "People before projects, and projects before people's stuff." Our relationships with one another were the wellspring of our service, so they were more important than our projects. But our service to the world was more important than spending time with someone rehashing the same old personal issues (that is, *stuff*).

Decision-making and Leadership

Our decision-making process was based on several underlying guiding principles. We would ask, "Does this fit our shared vision and purpose?" We attempted to be guided by an overall ring of rightness, not by our individual preferences. Only in the absence of a clear answer would we bow to a strong opinion. So it was really a decision-listening process rather than a decision-making one. Our goal was mutual surrender to this ring of rightness.

We had a fluid leadership style, even though we had a visionary leader in Joe. We deliberately surrendered our will to whoever in that moment was clearly the leader by virtue of articulating a clear vision, having expertise, being tuned into a person or situation, being in charge of a particular duty, or by agreement. Leadership came to the one who had the best bead on the subject and knew how to get the job done, or didn't know but was eager to learn. One or another of us would step up to be leader when we felt an internal sense that this was ours to do.

Each person was both leader and worker, whatever helped implement our shared vision. At one time or another, every one of us got a chance to lead, just as everyone got a chance to follow. As leaders, we strove for clarity, dispassion, and integrity. As followers, we strove for full understanding, surrender, and joy thorough the execution of tasks. In the bigger picture, we knew we were all dancing together.

Some examples come to mind: Monica headed up the FI Speaker's Bureau, Marcia's leadership took the form of being a scout and bringing home ideas and tools from other organizations, and Marilynn organized mass mailings of our promotional materials to our whole FI network.

One day, Diane came home from her job at IBM (where she was working toward financial independence) and reported that they were accepting grant proposals for new IBM computers. Since personal desktop computers were not common yet, we realized this was our best way to get the computer we needed for doing the ALS study. I ended up being the project lead in the following way, as described in my journal:

> *When I sat down to work on the grant proposal, I didn't think I would have anything to offer, but suddenly I had a clear vision that it needed to be done as a scientific grant proposal. Since I had the clear vision and the know-how, and since I communicated the vision clearly, I became the leader, although I thought I could just hand the job over to someone else to flesh out and they could be leader. It was like everybody climbed aboard my train because it was going in the right direction and made me conductor! For me, it was my best example of being flexible, letting go of my agenda, going with the flow, and even enjoying a lot of it.*

We got the computer and used it throughout the course of the ALS study.

Vicki and I became co-leaders on various writing projects. We were so different, and perhaps that was what made us a good team. She could articulate the concepts both verbally and in writing. I could organize the material into a logical structure and cut the unnecessary fluff. Sometimes I knew what needed to be said, and she knew how to say it. This was true for the white paper on overconsumption we wrote for the League of Women Voters, so we co-led that project.

When I stepped in to help with analyzing the data for the ALS Project, no one asked me to be a leader. I saw a need and realized my background as a scientist gave me the skills to do this and learn whatever I didn't know.

Clear Communication and Coordination

Clear communication was essential to all aspects of our work—among ourselves and with other people and organizations. Joe had the image that NRM was like a starfish. We depended on our sensory organs (one another) to tell us which direction to move next, when to put out the left foot, when to put out the right, when to withdraw. We had to trust one another to give accurate information about what we should do next—as an individual and as an organism.

Usually, those who were most articulate were our spokespeople. Joe and Vicki were our primary communicators. They had very different styles, but both were facile with words and concepts. We were a communal organism, and we strove to be of one mind—not in the sense of giving away our power but reaching something close to a group consensus. Because we were of one mind, we allowed our best communicators to do the talking, and we spoke as one voice. The object was to communicate, not *who* communicated.

I had trouble describing what I saw; I got it intellectually, but putting it into words didn't come easily. So I chose to be a spokesperson only when I was clearly the authority or when those more articulate weren't present. If I never said a word in an evening with guests, though, I would be actively listening, not daydreaming or bored (usually), and all parties could feel that my energy was totally present. I would pipe up if I saw something missing or in need of elaboration or clarification. To some observers or guests, some of us might have seemed invisible, but we were actively engaged and feeding energy into the conversation.

Some of us started an optional weekly practice session we called Table Topics. The idea was to talk extemporaneously about common topics that would come up over the dinner table with guests. Actually, this was mainly for my benefit because I had such a hard time speaking off the cuff. Give me time to think it through or write it down and I'm okay, but not in the moment. I dreaded these Sunday afternoon practice sessions. I also took a weekly improvisation class for six months with the same goal, and it was one of the hardest things I've ever done. These efforts did help a little bit, but public speaking would never be my forte. Fortunately, I had other skills and qualities I could offer the group.

It was essential that we stay connected at the "do" level so that we were coordinated and moving as one organism in our work. To that end, we had endless meetings to ensure this group coherence. In addition to our daily morning gathering (with Sunday being optional), we had business meetings almost every evening.

Frequent debriefing kept us on track. After an event or a social engagement, we would review with a clear eye our individual and group participation and decision-making, and evaluate what did and didn't work and what could have been done better or communicated more clearly. In this way, we learned from our mistakes and could adjust our course of action or follow up if needed. Of course, we strove to be as free from ego as possible in this process, reminding ourselves that we wanted to serve in the best way possible.

Looking Out for the Whole and Personal Freedom

Another key to the well-oiled machine was setting aside our personal agendas for the well-being of the whole. When needed, we sacrificed a sense of separate self for the "we." We were a collective, and we were in service to the collective will. Obviously, we each had to be powerful contributors in cocreating that collective will for this to be a healthy practice. We trained ourselves that if we tended to the whole, our needs would be met too—a fierce practice to be selfless without being a patsy. Vicki said, "If we can bring this learning forward of how to live in community, how to relinquish your own little agenda for the well-being of the whole, this is the lesson of our time."

There was a fine balance between looking out for the whole and personal freedom, and we didn't always get it right. When Monica felt called to do volunteer work in prisons, some of us were not very supportive because it took energy away from our other projects. In hindsight, I rue not supporting Monica in doing something that she was gifted at and that brought her respect and appreciation from those she served, plus a sense of aliveness and tremendous satisfaction. Fortunately, she went ahead and volunteered in prison anyway, through the Alternatives to Violence Project, and has made a difference in the lives of countless inmates for decades.

Most of us ended up sacrificing many of our own desires and callings for the good of the whole and putting on hold other parts of ourselves that wanted expression but didn't fit into the well-oiled machine. We would discover just how much this was true as our community began its process of unweaving later on.

Each bee does what needs to be done to move the colony forward. How utterly divine that they put the colony first. Imagine if we did that; imagine if each day, we put our best self forward and did whatever it is our community—local or global—requires to keep the world going in a way that supports all life. Could we be so brave and generous?[3]

[A] true community is a covenant made in free-willing surrender and sacrifice...The secret of community lies in the freedom of self-determination, in the personal decision of each member to surrender to the whole and, at the same time, to exercise his will for the good.[4]

Power and Empowerment

Empowerment was an important word in our vocabulary, and we used it in a couple of different ways. Our work was focused on empowering people (i.e., helping them see that they have the power) to take responsibility for their lives in the areas of finances, health, and relationships by offering tools and new ways of thinking—that is, new road maps.

[3]Freeman, Jacqueline. *Song of Increase: Listening to the Wisdom of Honeybees for Kinder Beekeeping and a Better World.* (Boulder, Colo.: Sounds True, 2016), 11.
[4]Arnold, Eberhard. *Why We Live in Community.* (Walden, N.Y.: Plough Publishing House, 1995), 16,18.

In our family, we embraced the notion that we were each powerful individuals, able to access and use our own power for the good of ourselves and others. We empowered one another by sharing tools, perceptions, ways of thinking, and feedback, and by helping one another be more powerful human beings in as many ways as we could.

We also used empowerment in a slightly different but equally important way. To empower someone was to recognize their unique gifts and pave the way for them to offer these gifts to others and the world. To offer empowerment was to convey your trust and support, to add your blessings to their endeavors, or to create a space for them to step into. For example, it might have been as simple as someone conveying to me that they trusted me to take the lead on a given project. Or someone might have introduced me to a visitor in a way that conveyed my unique value and their respect for me.

Sometimes resentments, fears, jealousies, or simply inattentiveness would keep us from wholeheartedly empowering someone else. But this form of empowerment was our goal and the key to our synergy, so we stayed alert to ways we could empower one another. Still, we missed many opportunities.

Of course, no amount of empowerment matters if you don't *claim* or *use* your power—i.e., have enough self-confidence and self-respect to use your gifts. I saw this clearly for myself when we were doing an exercise called Lost At Sea that I had requested for my birthday. We divided into two teams and were told that there had been a shipwreck and we were lost at sea in a rubber life raft with the others in our group. We were tasked with prioritizing the fifteen items that were saved from the shipwreck. Our group's chance of survival depended upon ranking these items in their order of importance. We first prioritized these items individually and then had to come to a consensus as a group on the final order. In the discussion about priorities, I allowed myself to be swayed by others with strong opinions and didn't share a particular piece of knowledge I had. It turned out that my knowledge was key, and because I had held back, we lost to the other team. So I have learned to more readily step forward with my insights and good ideas.

Cocreation

We liked the term *cocreation* to describe how we worked together because it emphasized the *co* aspect of the word. Something was created by our efforts together that no one individual could create. We lived in a group-created soup of ideas, creativity, liveliness, and blue-sky thinking. Our morning gathering, especially, was a time to bring up new insights and ideas about our work or our spiritual journey. Someone might say, "Hey, I was just thinking, and maybe we could . . ." Someone else would add, "Yes, and we could . . ." Pretty soon, a potential action or form emerged from this creative building off one another. No one of us could have come up with this by ourselves; many different people were required to generate it.

In this way, most of our products, such as the tape course, our book, and our various pamphlets were cocreations. Because each of us was involved in the creation, we all got to *own* and take credit for them.

Collaboration with Others

Collaboration was a critical piece to making the well-oiled machine hum, and we collaborated with other individuals and groups whenever and however we could. There were our wider circle of friends and family, our volunteers, and our network of FIers and people who had listened to our tape course or read *Your Money or Your Life*. There were also our colleagues in dozens of other groups and organizations who were working toward a sustainable future for our world. We sought ways to work, often invisibly, alongside them to help make their conference, meeting, campaign, report, network, or project something that maximally served the world. Sometimes this took the form of pitching in to help them, other times we donated money, still others we offered learnings from our own experience or we connected them to other colleagues in our network.

In turn, we were inspired, changed, loved, challenged, held, and supported by these friends, colleagues, and organizations. The energy traveling back and forth provided a feedback loop. For example, we might receive a letter from someone whose life had been changed by doing our FI course, and this would feed more energy into the loop. This promoted synergy among us and also among organizations.

Many of our collaborators and colleagues were also visionaries, and I would be inspired by the picture they were painting of the future or of the ways they were bringing change to the world. Something in me would relax and feel deeply reassured, knowing that there were so many individuals and organizations out there just like ours doing their part to bring change and enable transformation.

Celebration and Recognition

A Tibetan Buddhist concept that we took to heart was, "Recognition is the key to liberation." Recognition, in this sense, meant recognizing when you've accomplished something—it could be a project or a piece of a project, or it could be a shift in your inner state. Once this accomplishment was recognized, a sense of freedom often rushed in.

We also put a high value on recognizing and honoring one another's accomplishments and our group accomplishments. We would tell the story of how it had come about, acknowledge the high and low points, the wins and losses, and allow the group enthusiasm to infuse us with fresh energy to continue moving toward our purpose.

One celebration stands out for me because it was initiated by good friends of ours—our family doctor and his wife. We always enjoyed lively conversation and happy heartfelt exchanges about our lives when we were with them. One time, they invited all ten of us to their house for a salmon dinner to celebrate the publishing of *Your Money or Your Life*. It was quite an undertaking to fete a group such as ours, and it meant a lot to me that they would do that. They proceeded to draw out of us the whole story of how the book had been published and what each of us had contributed to it. I have warm memories to this day of that special evening.

Chapter 9

Our Spiritual Foundation

Most spiritual seekers and practitioners will be familiar with the spiritual tenets that were foundational to how our group operated—they aren't new. But living and working with other people committed to living them on a daily basis and holding one another accountable brought these concepts into sharp focus for us.

Belief in Some Kind of Higher Power
Each of us, at our core, believed in some type of Higher Power, something larger than ourselves. A few of us called this God, but more commonly, we called it the Universe or Spirit. Some called it Universal Mind or The Unknown. And of course, our term of endearment for God: Lola. We found we could easily shift back and forth between these terms and translate into our favored terminology if need be.

"Early on a Mountain Morning . . ."
(By Monica, the day the group left beautiful Mount Lemmon, Arizona, to go on the road in the just-completed UV)

early on a mountain morning
you can hear birds sing.
early on a mountain morning

you can hear truth ring.
ringin' out the song of love,
singin' of the glory.
It touches me and I can see—
that everything is holy.

Consciousness and Transformation

Consciousness—that is, being awake and aware of how life really works—was foundational. As you probably know from your own experience, waking up isn't so hard—it's staying awake that is difficult. We wake up again and again to broader views of reality. We go back to sleep, slipping into old, unconscious, habitual patterns of doing things. Then something, some kind of pain or suffering or some inner impulse, prods us to wake up again. We choose and rechoose to hike up the mountain and not slide back down. This process could be called continually passing in and out of "sainthood" (that is, waking up and falling asleep). Since we all have that potential, Evy once did a sharing on "I am Buddha, and you are too." Well, yes and no. But why not strive for that? Decide to be Buddha in your own life and then become aware of when you are stepping into and out of "Buddhahood."

Transformation was what we were aiming for, the prize we had our eyes on. We were committed to living more and more in an awakened state where we could see reality clearly and spend less time being stuck in outdated ways of thinking.

One key was to be open to reframing our experience. For example, two people sitting on the edge of a cliff watching a sunset could have very different experiences. One could be totally present with the sunset and remember the glory of it. The other could be ruminating about something or trembling in fear of falling off the cliff and totally miss the sunset. By expanding our consciousness, we can experience both simultaneously or choose to experience heaven instead of hell. We have the power to create our experience of reality—in this case, our experience of the sunset. I reminded myself that the kingdom of heaven is indeed at hand: inside me!

Our Divinity

We believed in the divinity of every being—that spark of goodness and beauty that lies within each of us, even if it's hard to find. The Quakers call it "that of God." Our objective was to see the sacred in one another, to relate to the divinity in one another, not to our small, ego selves. We sought to deeply respect one another for who we were, with nothing of ourselves (our small, ego selves) in the way.

When I met the UV Family, they related to me from their divinity to my divinity. Joe would say something like, "Remember, magnificence is your birthright, not your potential. Don't sell yourself short. You are perfect the way you are." This was a totally new concept for me. But over time, I could begin to recognize and finally embrace my own divinity.

It was as if each of us was a perfect jewel, and our task was to scrape the dirt (the accumulation of our human failings) off so that we could live more and more from our jewel selves.

The Secret of Life
By Joe Dominguez

The secret of life is simply you . . .
your magnificence, your divinity.
Love is the medium through which
the divinity manifests.
The medium is the message.
Love is the message.
When you love, you are carrying the message . . .
You are manifesting your magnificence,
your divinity.
When you feel love, you feel good.
When you feel good, you feel love.
When you feel good, you feel god.
When you feel god, you feel good.
Love is your creation.
Your natural state is

the ecstatic experience of Love.
It is simply the conscious experience
of our aliveness, made manifest . . . shared.
Love does not "happen" to us.
We happen it.
We happen it by removing that which blocks it.
Living a life is simply the process of removing
those barriers to experiencing Love.

Love, Compassion, and Inclusivity

We wanted our lives together to be rooted in Spirit and love. We sought to be in partnership with Spirit. And we sought to live in and come from the space of love—that is, "I am the source of love. Love is unconditional and nondirectional."

Vicki recalls:

> By love, we meant that spacious, respectful relationship with "the other"—be it a person, nature, or the universe. It is being with another with nothing of one's own in the way. If you leave your fears and even your hopes at the door, you enter a space called love. By love, we also meant utter transparency—being with another with everything of one's own in the engagement.

We asked ourselves, "How can I love?" It was a process of choosing love over and over again—letting go of the small self and stepping into the larger self. We tried to make our day-to-day decisions from a loving place. Our community was built on this foundation of love.

And we stretched ourselves to include others in our love. Inclusivity was a key attitude we aspired to bring to all our relationships. It could look like being intentional about bringing a new friend home so we could all meet them. Or it could be an open-hearted welcoming of a guest or colleague who was visiting us.

Compassion, a corollary of love, was also a really important quality that we cultivated in ourselves. This was a quality of kindness and caring that was not about pitying or being virtuous. A large part of compassion was simply listening and being present with another person.

We also practiced tough love when necessary. When someone was in the small self for an extended period of time—e.g., being grumpy, critical, angry, or fearful—they were denying their divinity. In this case, gentle compassion might not work. Sometimes the most effective way to help that person get unstuck was to *boot* them up to the larger self. Usually, all of us could see the stuckness, and whoever felt they had something to offer and had a high level of trust with the person who was stuck would step forward. Monica did this for me once when I was deeply entrenched in my own reactions of judgment and feeling buffeted by everyone else. It was not fun to be the recipient of this energy, but it helped me get unstuck. It does take deep trust and respect for the one who does the booting, or you can merely feel unjustly picked on.

Sometimes, all it took to open my heart and help me return to a loving place when I was being judgmental was for someone to reach out to me with a simple hug. This worked much better than if they had avoided me or responded with criticism.

At other times, when I would be overwhelmed by all I thought I needed to be doing, someone would point out to me that no matter what you *think* your current job is, your *only* job is putting more love out into the world. If you're not doing that while you're doing your so-called job, you're not really doing the job. The trick is to *recognize* when you're not putting love out and correct it on the spot so that the time when you're just enslaved to your list or being judgmental is as short as possible.

Service

Service was a foundational aspect of our work. Our lives were lived in the context of service—that is, putting love out into the world. The projects we did we could do because we were standing on the foundation of love, the love and caring we shared with one another. Service arose from the fullness of our relationship with one another, not out of duty or to compensate for deficiency, but out of joyful connection among ourselves. It was a spirit of generosity and voluntary giving.

We recognized there were degrees of service. False service was doing good for personal gain, power, prestige, fame, or brownie points with God. Conditional service was doing good out of duty or to fulfill the expectations of a role—because you were a mother, a member of the church, or some other role. True service was doing for others without hidden personal motives or undue concern for yourself. (That is, concern beyond what was necessary for your health and well-being.) It was "responding to whatever is needed and wanted" (Werner Erhard's phrase), serving Gaia (the living planet Earth), serving the world. A key question we would ask ourselves is, "How does this serve?" For example, "How does this action I am about to take serve?" or "How does it serve for me to be grumpy?" or "How does this new project we want to undertake serve?"

When I first met the UV Family, I had a narrow concept of what service was—for example, volunteering in a nursing home—and I simply wasn't interested. Over the next several years as I pitched in with everyone, my definition of service expanded to include simple acts of giving, listening to the open-reel tapes of Joe's seminars in Jenner, or just observing where my energy was needed and then providing it. By then, there were so many ways I wanted to serve that I didn't have time for them all.

True service was service without expectation of return—both in terms of results and taking credit for results. We adopted a familiar saying: "You can accomplish anything if you're willing to take credit for nothing." This is a fierce practice! Since I was usually a background person in our group, I seldom got credit for our publications, and this felt fine to me. But when it came to the ALS Project, I struggled with this concept and finally acknowledged that I wanted to be listed as a coauthor on our major paper. I think the request came from a place of self-esteem and claiming my rightful place in that big body of work, and I don't regret it.

We coined the term "maid service" for doing something from a place of low self-esteem or lack in yourself. It could look like true service—that is, with nothing of yourself in the way. But if the motivation came from feeling unworthy or not whole in yourself, then your service would be colored by that and look like kowtowing.

I wandered in and out of true service over the course of any day. The trick was to notice when I'd slipped out of it.

Surrender, Trust, and Courage

These three keys to life worked together, and through any one of them you could find the others if you had fallen off the path.

Trust and surrender were like two sides of the same coin. Surrender involved letting go of our own ideas, agendas, and preferences; listening to Lola; and embracing what we heard. As Seng Ts'an, the 3rd Patriarch of Zen, said, "The Great Way is not difficult for those who have no preferences." What a simple but profound statement. Imagine how many preferences we each have during any day and how many we are willing to let go of instead of being run by. We would remind ourselves of this saying when things got challenging or when we got unexpected dancing lessons from God.

I put it this way in my diary: "Doing what is wanted and needed takes surrendering to the will of God and also to the will of the whole. When doing what is needed and wanted, I'm in the flow of the Universe, and my life works." It required trusting that if you give your life over to God, you will get what you need. Surrender wasn't about being submissive or giving up—it was a powerful choice, not coming from a sense of defeat.

That didn't mean surrender was always easy. I had an ongoing conversation with my to-do list that would go something like this: "Oh God, I can't get this done. I didn't get to that. I'll never be able to finish . . ." Then too much "hurry worry" would set in. Whereas, if I could surrender and trust that everything that needed to would get done in right timing, then I could relax. I would often rail against "what is" instead of accepting and loving the way it is and not being attached to a particular way life should look. Expectations or thinking there's a way things ought to be ended in my unhappiness.

For our relationships with one another to work well, we needed to trust one another deeply. This kind of trust developed over time, the result of many small and not so small interactions and spending one-on-one time with one another. We also learned to trust ourselves as we got internal and external feedback that we were on the right track.

Life worked better when we trusted in the mysterious unfolding of the Universe, when we cooperated with the unknown. This meant going with the flow, not fighting the current of how life was unfolding in any given minute, and knowing that things work for the good.

I was prone to resisting the flow. One day, I discovered a flat tire on the car that several of us drove. Joe pointed out that having a working car was more important than anything else I wanted to do that day. But I was loath to drop my agenda to fix the flat, and I put up quite a fight internally before I grudgingly took the time to fix the tire. To this day, I call that lesson to mind when, for example, something in my material world breaks that should be fixed now, and I set aside my agenda with less grumbling.

Surrender and trust required courage. Courage to step into the unknown. Courage to trust in yourself and in others. Courage to surrender to something outside yourself. Courage to make space for something new to show up in your life. Courage to trust that it would all work out. Courage to live from your best self. As Vicki said, "It took courage to break free from encumbering concepts, practices, possessions ... to express our essence, our core selves, and beliefs, fully and with authenticity."

Before deciding to move into our Seattle house, Marilynn did the deepest soul-searching of her life. Committing to living with all of us was like "jumping off a mountaintop with nothing for a safety net. It was outside the box of the known." This is the kind of courage I'm talking about. Reflecting on that experience, Marilynn says, "I've been faced with taking that leap many times since. And because of that initial one, I have always taken it."

Marcia showed such courage as she was trying to get clarity about an inner prompting to move away from Seattle. Vicki told her, "You are marching to the drum of Spirit with such faith. To hear such a call ... takes very careful discernment ... I can imagine you turning this decision over and over, looking for the blindnesses, the attachments, the source of the leading, the affirmations from the outer that the choice is true." After applying her careful discernment, Marcia surrendered to her inner knowing and made the move.

Joy, Gratitude, and Lightening Up

Joy and gratitude were also two sides of the same coin. One engendered the other. We subscribed to the saying, "The attitude of gratitude brings altitude." And if one of us was feeling down, someone might list all the things we could be grateful for. As we counted our blessings, our spirits would often rise. Approaching the world with awe and wonder also fed into the gratitude and joy.

An attitude of relaxing and lightening up could be the doorway to joy and gratitude. It was one of the hardest things for me to do. But I had plenty of help from those around me who were always reminding me to lighten up. From my diary:

> The more fully one participates in Life, the more joy one experiences. (This has been true for me over the past year or so.) I am experiencing more and more joy as a result of more fully participating, which requires being flexible, available, surrendered, coming from "plate empty" instead of "plate full." Participation in Life is a moment-by-moment choice = be here now. Am I participating now? And now? And now?

Whenever we go with the flow, we lighten up. And when we lighten up, it's easier to go with the flow.

To help us not take ourselves too seriously, when one of us would complain in a poor-me kind of way, someone might say, "Oh, poor baby. Oh, poopsie." We would be taking the chance that the complainer wouldn't take offense but would perhaps laugh at themselves and gain some perspective to see that their situation wasn't all that bad if they could just lighten up about it.

Form and Essence

A useful concept for me was the distinction between form and essence. *Form* is tangible, something you can see, feel, or touch, or a concept that can be described—e.g., house, job, mate, or nonprofit organization. *Essence* is the spirit or core or intrinsic nature of something or someone, their defining quality.

Most useful change occurs at the level of essence, not form. If the form isn't working, then rather than manipulating it, step back into the life-giving essence. Once the essence is clear, the right new form will emerge.

As Joe would paraphrase Werner Erhard in the FI course, life works when you go from Be (essence) to Do (taking action) to Have (resulting form). Embody the essence of FI (have a clear vision of what you want, imagine what it would take—for example, integrity and responsibility), take the appropriate action to live out this vision, and becoming FI will be the result.

Time and time again, I would find myself struggling with an outdated form, having totally forgotten to go back to essence. For example, when Evy and I would have a difference of opinion about how to move forward on the ALS data analysis, if we remembered to step back into why we were doing the project and what we were trying to accomplish, we could usually find the way forward. So not being attached to form and hanging on to essence (the core) was a fundamental guiding principle in our personal lives and our work.

Choice

A basic spiritual tenet was that you always have choice. Choice about how you respond to what life throws your way. Choice to step into love when you feel judgmental, for example. "Just choose it!" was a common reminder in our group. We could choose to be high, to be happy, to stay awake to reality. Monica's song says it best.

"Choose It"
By Monica

> *Anger's got you in its grip, and it's driving you insane*
> *And those nasty thoughts are screaming 'round your brain*
> *You're wanting some relief but you don't know how to do it*
> *Well, I can tell you how, babe—you can simply choose it!*

Choose it . . . (choose the way you want to feel) . . . Choose it
Choose it . . . you can go ahead and . . . Choose it
If you want to be enlightened and you want to be happy
Just choose it!

When the world is looking gloomy and you're feeling all alone
Your partner calls you stupid and your self-esteem's way down
So you're looking to your friends, or to some god up above
But the answer's in your heart—you can simply choose love

Choose it . . . (choose the way you want to be) . . . Choose it
Choose it . . . you can go ahead and . . . Choose it
If you want to be enlightened and you want to be happy
Just choose it!

You're searching for enlightenment and looking for the way
You eat brown rice and meditate every single day
You've taken all the workshops and you've read the holy books
But you just can't seem to get it—life ain't how it oughta look
. . .

So, choose it . . . (just the way it is) . . . Choose it
Choose it . . . you can go ahead and . . . Choose it
If you want to be enlightened and you want to be happy
Just choose it!

A distinction between *process* and *choice* was useful. Going through a process to achieve something was effective in the physical and mental domains. But in the emotional and spiritual domains, process didn't seem to work as well—only choice did.

Joe's analogy went something like this: When you feel up against something emotional or spiritual, it feels like a wall in front of you (the more fearful you are, the bigger the wall), so the temptation is to go through a process to get over or around the wall. Eventually, the process leads you right back to the same point (the wall). In reality, the wall is just a line you can easily step over by declaration alone—this is called choice. No matter how many different processes you go through, you will come back to the same line (choice). On the other side of the line is "sainthood."

I had a huge learning about choice that I called Old Story/New Story. It happened one time when I was in distress over something that didn't work out the way I had wanted it to. I realized I could list in one column aspects of the dilemma and the hurt, sadness, and judgment I was experiencing and why it wasn't fair. Then in a side-by-side column, I could list a new story—how this incident might look from a different point of view, one that was more loving, empowering, and happy for me. I called the left-hand column the Old Story and the right-hand column the New Story. The breakthrough was the realization that it was simply a choice as to which story I wanted to be living. Wow. So simple, yet so profound.

What I discovered was that I had to constantly rechoose that new story. Here's what I wrote in my diary:

> It requires a commitment to choose the New Story every time. And that requires a knowing that the new story is worth any price. It requires a vision. You have to recognize the old habit patterns and then remember to choose something else. The old and new story are parallel realities. On this piece of paper, the two stories are side by side, and I get to choose which one I live in.

I ended up cutting the paper down the middle and throwing the left half in the wastebasket. The test was whether I could keep from retrieving it! I resolved that for every old story, I would create a new story based on love.

Honestly, here I am so many years later, nowhere near mastery of process versus choice at the emotional level. Sometimes choice seems elusive. I often wander through a process until I can find the switch inside me that is ready to choose to step back into love and then flip the switch.

Chapter 10

Our Community Guiding Principles

We considered ourselves a spiritual family, what Buddhists call a sangha. We were committed to supporting one another in coming from our highest natures. We used one another to grow spiritually: being one another's teachers and offering support in going beyond the small self and following a spiritual path. Our life together was a spiritual path in and of itself—living and working in harmony with nine other people and seeing what needed to be done and doing it minute by minute, day by day.

"Rules" of Our Community

While we had developed our own way of doing things, we didn't exactly have rules. But I would say we created our own Rule—a rule of how life works and how we wanted to live our lives. It was within the restriction of these rules that we found our freedom to love, to serve, and to make a difference. Living the spiritual principles *was* part of our Rule as were the following aspects.

Commitment

Commitment was essential to creating a cohesive circle, a community. Each of us was totally committed—to one another and to supporting one another's highest natures, to being true to ourselves, to living our values, to our vision, and to our work. We were committed to getting ourselves out of the way. Each of us did what needed to be done to move ourselves, our community, our vision, and our work forward.

We were also committed to bringing out the magnificence in one another (our inner light). Joe said it this way: "I love you and support you in being your highest self until death do us part or eternity, whichever comes first." We could count on one another. We had one another's backs.

Integrity, Accountability, Responsibility, and Honesty

We valued integrity. Being authentic was important, our actions being consistent with our words and beliefs. We held ourselves and one another accountable for our actions. We aspired to competence and impeccability. Our code phrase was "No leeway"—that is, no wiggle room to not do your best. Of course there were times when we *didn't* do our best, and we would clean up our mistakes, learn from them, and move on.

We believed we lived in an interconnected world where "We are One." So we took responsibility for ourselves, one another, and the world. We realized that we were responsible for every moment of our lives. And since all our actions have ripples (consequences), we took responsibility for the ripples too in all areas of our lives. Taking responsibility for our lives was not to be misconstrued as blame (being at fault) for hardships in our lives or meaning we had to go it alone without loving support. This kind of responsibility meant that we were each in the driver's seat of our own life, regardless of what had befallen us or might in the future. We could choose our attitude, and we could choose how we responded. It was empowering.

Our ethic was total honesty and willing self-disclosure. No secrets. Nothing arising in me that I was not willing to share, and no secrets between us. Anything said to one person could be repeated to others in the community, respectfully. This was sometimes hard on the person who divulged something to just one person, only to have it repeated to others, but we had to trust that this would bring greater clarity and understanding to whatever had been divulged. We tried not to sweep things big or small under the carpet. I tried to be brave enough to bring up things that troubled me, and I often experienced a wave of relief as the burden of my fear or concern was brought into the light to be witnessed and held by others.

Even though we were committed to living this way, later on, we saw with painful clarity ways that we had fallen far short of this ethic of total honesty and no secrets. But during the heyday of the well-oiled machine, we didn't realize this.

Communication and Deep Listening

Real communication requires deep listening. It also requires the capacity to reflect on oneself, on one another, and on the group. Our aim was to have deep conversation whenever possible—among ourselves, and also with friends, guests, and colleagues. We used every chance we could get to model a new way of being and relating to other people.

Listening—really listening—to someone took intention and practice. We trained ourselves to focus on what the person speaking was saying. Not thinking about how I was going to respond, not letting myself get distracted by other thoughts, ideas, or my current concerns. Just totally being there, taking in this other person—what they were saying, how they were saying it, their body language. When I could give someone my 100 percent attention, when I was there for them, ideally they would experience me being totally present, receiving without judgment what they were saying. Because I sometimes had no idea how to respond to them, simply being present was my gift to them.

Some guests were distinctly uncomfortable having ten people totally focused on them, deeply listening—it wasn't in their body of experience. Other people just wanted to be heard, and that was enough. Into that space of pure, loving listening, some people would pour their hearts out, saying things they'd never divulged or even admitted to themselves before. It also tended to bring out an honest appraisal. Often, they would feel deeply seen, perhaps for the first time in their lives.

This was true for me when I met the UV Family at Dinosaur National Monument. I found that when someone was really listening to me—without fidgeting, looking at their watch, daydreaming, or yawning—I felt connected to them and like I mattered.

Remembering past conversations and the important events in that person's life, especially their spiritual life, was part of deeply listening. We learned how to relate in detail conversations we'd just had and remember enough to pick up where we had left off the next time we were with them, whether it was a family member, a friend, or a guest.

Listening as if nothing else in the world matters is a rigorous spiritual practice.

Attunement and Maintaining Connections

Being a cohesive, tightly connected group was essential to our success. To accomplish this, we needed to stay connected to Spirit and purpose, and remain connected at the heart level with ourselves and everyone else in the community. We needed to stay in tune, to be attuned to one another. In *Your Resonant Self: Guided Meditations and Exercises to Engage Your Brain's Capacity for Healing*, Sarah Peyton defines attunement as "the experience of someone focusing on us with warmth, respect, and curiosity. This person wonders what it is like to be us, using all available human sensitivities to tune in to us." We strove for this kind of experience with one another as often as possible.

We were in constant touch with one another through our daily and weekly rituals, and we were expert at seeing a need and pitching in, usually with enthusiasm. Our weekly Family Night was a reflective space where we caught up with one another at a deeper level. Heart Sharing was our communal prayer and meditation, a way to tune in to Spirit, a way to connect with and tune in to one another. This ritual not only kept us connected physically, emotionally, intellectually, and spiritually, but also provided ways to digest experience and information.

We also made it a priority to stay connected by consciously creating one-on-one times (talks, walks, sexual intimacy). As Monica says, "These one-to-one relationships were the building blocks of the community." We often reflected back to each other who we knew them to be, holding them to that, holding the space for that even if they were depressed and couldn't see their highest self.

When Lynn reflects on our years together, one thing that stands out is the one-on-one walks and talks. Building those relationships with each of us was precious to her. She remembers conversations about sex, about creativity and how to nurture it, and how to create healthy relationships.

Marcia and I relished what we called our at-the-beach days where we would sit on the beach along Puget Sound and allow ourselves to roll around big topics. For example, one of our ongoing explorations regarded the relationship between *being* and *doing*, and how to find the right balance in our lives. Marcia called these "very wonderful times of spacious sharing and dreaming."

When Monica and I spent time together, a conversation with her might go something like this:

Monica: "How are you—really?"

Me, bursting into tears: "I'm upset because I had a confusing interaction with so-and-so."

Monica would then draw me out more on this subject and help me gain a different perspective.

Me: "And what about you, Monica?"

Monica: "I've been working on being more mindful. I want to be more aware and focused on what I'm doing in the present moment, without getting distracted or caught up in my thoughts so much that I stop paying attention to what I'm doing and get sloppy."

Me: "How can I support you in doing that? Is there something I can say to you when I see that happening?"

This note from Lynn to me was another way someone could offer reflection and maintain connection: "I haven't known how to tell you this—still don't—so I'll tell you anyway. Thank you for letting me work at your desk a couple of weeks ago. As many times as I've been in your room, I've never *seen* you as I did that day, sitting at your desk among the things you choose to surround you. I sensed there something so tender, delicate, so truly feminine . . . I've known for a long time you are beautiful. It's a joy to be discovering ever more depth of that beauty . . . I love you, Lynn."

Sometimes a particularly close bond would develop between two members. I think of Monica and Vicki's relationship. Even though they had very different natures, their ongoing closeness since the Mexico days and their sharing an office together created a special intimacy and bond that provided a behind-the-scenes foundation that we all benefited from. One of their rituals was having "candle time" in their office before dinner—a chance to pause and savor the day.

When one or more of us were out of town, we tried to stay tuned in via phone calls and letters. The *home team* provided grounding and support for the *away team*, whether that individual or group was away for personal or work-related reasons.

These were all ways we tended the collective.

Working Through Differences

We had very different personalities, and based on that alone, we probably wouldn't have chosen one another. But our spiritual connection and commitment to something higher made these differences seem, if not insignificant, at least manageable. We had to learn to accept one another's foibles and particular character traits. This was not easy, and personality clashes still happened. It was a hard lesson for me to learn that I couldn't count on changing other people, that my real point of leverage was changing myself and my reactions. And the recognition that our diverse natures were essential to our work and contributed to our heartbeat.

Expressing emotions was problematic. Joe supported the concept that feelings weren't real and shouldn't be indulged in. "Aspire to *have* emotions, not be *had* by them," he'd say. Monica would say that that was all well and good, but that feelings needed to be acknowledged and expressed. While these two approaches don't have to be contradictory, the lack of clarity and consistency about how to handle emotions led to confusion about what to do when they arose. I often struggled with my emotions and when to express them and when to work with them by myself. I spent a lot of time being *had* by my emotions without being able to find the switch or key to gain a perspective where I could just *have* them.

Of course, unresolved emotions could easily muddy the waters in our interpersonal relationships. We were committed to working through differences, even though there were times when we wanted to ignore, run away, avoid, or declare our "rightness" instead. Essential to resolving differences was taking responsibility for our reactions and being willing to communicate when something seemed amiss. I often had to remind myself that love was more important than being right.

Mirroring

An important aspect of our community was being mirrors for one another, reflecting back what we were seeing in someone. Sometimes we would be seeing a positive shift and want to mirror this new state of being. Sometimes we would want to describe a quality of theirs we were particularly appreciating. Other times we wanted to give feedback that some behavior, attitude, or action seemed like it was coming from their small self and offer an invitation to move into a higher state of consciousness.

We benefited from one another's insights and ways of being for our own enlightenment and transformation, and we helped one another through the hard parts. One of our mottos was, "Don't kill the messenger." In other words, take in the message and the love behind it, and thank the deliverer of this "bad" news about your behavior. One advantage of a group was that if you didn't like the message, you could check it out with someone else. Usually, you'd find that everyone else could uncannily see this flaw that you alone were blind to. Excuses just muddied the waters and kept you from seeing it.

A challenge I had was that my mirroring was sometimes clouded by a carrier wave of judgment. So others couldn't hear the message I was trying to deliver—all they could hear was the judgment. I had to learn how to keep a neutral and useful observation from slipping into a negative judgment. The former would likely be heard and received, but not the latter.

At times we were oracles for one another. Sometimes this involved blurting out a truth that was obvious to everyone once it was said. One time, I said to Marcia, "Marcia, you're not thriving," and my saying that gave her permission to admit it to herself and begin to address her distress. Another time, later in our years together when our group was slowly disbanding, I blurted out in anguish, "Marilynn is leaving!" This outburst refocused our energy on making sure to give her the loving goodbye and good wishes she deserved. At other times, someone would share something during Family Night that would be the insight we all needed to hear right then.

Intimacy and Sexuality

Intimacy—emotional, spiritual, physical, and even mental—was another building block of our community. It meant staying in tune, caring, actively participating in another person's growth, and supporting them to be their highest selves. It might lead to sexual intimacy, and it might not, but the intention was to deepen our connection, not to have sex.

Joe elaborated on this:

> Intimacy is a choice, just like commitment is. You can choose to have everything you do be intimate, feel intimate, or you can choose to have certain actions represent the agreed-on expression of intimacy—for example, in our family, sexuality is just one of many agreed-on expressions of intimacy. You can choose to have working on the computer together be intimate. Or taking someone else into consideration when planning something that involves their time can be considered intimate.

Here was my take on the subject at that time (from my diary):

> Intimacy occurs (that is, one feels intimate) when one is being open, vulnerable, loving. So the objective is to be intimate all the time because

it's synonymous with being "in love" all the time, of being in the Heart Sharing space all the time. So what actions help one break down the blocks or lift the veil that prevents one from being open all the time?

A huge part of our intimacy and an essential part of our heartbeat was being physically demonstrative—especially with kisses and hugs, lots of hugs. The heartbeat could have been fueled by hugs alone. They communicated love, respect, caring, and a direct transmission of deep knowing and seeing the other. Not just any hug, but when both people were totally present, eye to eye, heart to heart, soul to soul, cherishing each other. There would be the perfunctory hugs or just blowing a kiss when we were too tired or in a hurry. But the let's-get-this-over-with kind of hugs were rare. A hug could also create an opening for more communication. For example, a well-timed hug could bring me to tears, and I'd have to fess up to what was bothering me.

Each of us had a distinctive hug, and I probably could guess who was hugging me with my eyes closed.

- Paula: light as a feather, like she didn't want to disturb my aura.
- Monica: in the bosom of the mother, conveying warmth and love.
- Joe: firm and sexual, implicit or explicit, swimming in his deep-brown eyes.
- Marilynn: joyful embrace.
- Marcia: caring and total acceptance.
- Evy: sometimes warm, sometimes playful (including a tickle), swinging her weakened arm around as best she could, sometimes perfunctory when she wasn't in the mood.
- Lynn: full-bodied and totally embraced.
- Vicki: happily wrapping me up in her enthusiasm with sometimes a quick back rub thrown in while I'm gazing into her bright, green-gray eyes.
- Diane: solid, grounded, cheerful.

- Me: almost always attentive, present, and caring; happy or sad, I could give a good hug.

Imagine this: twenty years of hugs, at least twice a day, times nine people, not including guests, equaled 131,400 hugs for each person. I do miss all those hugs.

The intimacy of sexual expression was also a key piece in our relationships. So how did this work in our household of ten? We had each been influenced by the sexual revolution created by access to the pill plus the breaking away from society's norms. It was a time of sexual freedom and experimentation. We were sexual in different pairings or groupings, and that was determined by the inclinations of those involved. Many of us were strictly heterosexual, while others explored same-sex relationships. Some people were more active sexually than others. There were no rules per se, but we shared a strongly held belief that the sexual act was a sacred act experienced by those involved and that ripples of this sacred act went out into the world as positive, healing energy. Expressing ourselves sexually was a beautiful and healing experience for many of us, an essential part of becoming whole and of loving ourselves. Each person, of course, had their own unique experience.

For me, expressing my love sexually was an important aspect of my life in this family—it added an extra dimension that was based not in my head but in my body and heart. And because our family provided such a safe container not bound by the restrictions of the larger culture and because of the sexual freedoms of the time, I stretched myself to explore possibilities I had not considered before. And my sexual relationship with Joe was important to my evolution. Without having the chance to develop that self-respect and self-love through seeing myself through a lover's eyes, I don't know how far I could have gone on the spiritual path and my quest for truth. I have deep gratitude for this gift from Joe.

Laughter, Fun, and Irreverence

There was always a vacillation between seriousness and irreverence, which kept us from taking ourselves and our mission too seriously.

Laughter was an essential component of the heartbeat. Puns, irony, absurdity, quips, raunchiness, making hamburger out of all sacred cows, slapstick—so many modes that elicited laughter. Irreverence and absurdity were hallmarks of our humor, and Joe, with his well-honed sense of the macabre, was often the instigator.

Watching Monty Python's film *The Meaning of Life* was a Rorschach test for newcomers like me. My lack of laughter and not understanding what was so funny said volumes about my deficits in humor. Other favorites of the group were Dr. Demento and George Carlin on the radio and the movie *Blazing Saddles*. Oh, and making fun of ourselves. Nothing was off limits. We had moments of pure zaniness and hilarity, like imitating Joe slapping a fly on his plate of spaghetti with a folded newspaper and spraying spaghetti all over the rest of us. Or the time all of us donned napkins on our heads at our picnic table under the fig tree to keep from getting purple droppings on our hair from the starlings gorging on the ripe figs. We also acted silly sometimes, like when Diane had us all do finger painting for her birthday celebration—what delightful fun, and what a mess.

All of this added a much needed lightness, especially for someone like me with a propensity for seriousness. Over the years, my sense of humor improved to the point that I dropped some pretty good one-liners myself.

My graduation in off-color humor came later after Joe died and Evy and Marilynn brought his ashes home from the mortuary. We didn't know what to do with them until we were ready to strew them in the desert, but Joe's desk seemed like the logical place. That first evening, some of us decided the box shouldn't just sit on his desk, kind of like an afterthought. So we put his special tapestry cap in bright blues and reds from Uzbekistan on top of the box and attached Joe's glasses to the front. The whole scene was so absurd and I was still so raw with grief that I doubled over in laughter and tears, rolling on the floor in my bathrobe. Joe would have liked that, I think. I had become a good student of his, being able to access humor in the face of despair. It helped in moving through the tough times. Macabre? Yes. Irreverent? Certainly. Healing? I think so. Honoring of who Joe was? Definitely.

Individual Work, Practice, and Renewal

Each of us was on our own spiritual path. We each believed in some kind of Higher Power, and we each had our own spiritual practices. We cultivated the capacity to reflect on ourselves. The guiding principles and group practices worked to the degree that each of us was committed to and doing the inner work we needed to do to keep our small selves out of the way. This might look like journaling, meditating, being out in nature, walking, talking with someone, reading supportive books, or listening to talks by spiritual teachers or recordings from our weekly Heart Sharings. Each of us did it our own way.

There was always the threat of so-called disappearing ink—forgetting an insight you once had. I found I could counteract this tendency by writing down my insights and telling them to others to reinforce them. Occasionally, I'd reread my diary and be reminded of insights I had much earlier that I had lost track of.

If you looked at my diary from those years, you would be struck by how much time I spent pondering or even brooding over various issues of communal life that were hard for me. There were issues with people whose personalities were very different from mine. As much as I loved and cherished Joe, there were aspects of his personality that were particularly difficult for me to live with, such as his direct, in-your-face brashness. There were also ways my needs weren't being met—needs for a quieter environment, more time in nature, more alone time, more sleep. And there was the angst of feeling like I wasn't being spiritual enough.

It would be many years later that I achieved enough clarity to see the cost of my striving and high expectations of myself. How harshly I judged myself! And I can see now how, in my striving to be a better person, I couldn't accept my failings and often lost sight of the joy in our lives together. Long after our group had disbanded, I read Stephen Levine's book *Who Dies?: An Investigation of Conscious Living and Conscious Dying* and stumbled upon his guided meditation on self-forgiveness. I would be in tears doing this meditation and realizing all the ways I had cast myself out of my heart during our years together.

For me, the joyful and compelling aspects of our lives together and my inner struggles always went hand in hand. Both threads were woven into my life with this family.

Creating the right balance in our lives and not burning out was something many of us struggled with—the dilemma of *be* time versus *do* time, personal time versus group time, work time versus renewal time.

We knew that renewal time was a necessary part of our work and that it enhanced productivity and creativity. We aimed to have our lives be an integrated whole, so that renewal time was incorporated into every day, with weekly and monthly renewal times as well. But going from theory to practice was not so easy. This was an ongoing challenge for me, and I never did find the right balance.

Time in nature was deeply nourishing for most of us, but we didn't do it as often as we would have liked. That being said, we managed to have fulfilling times in nature individually, in small groups, and collectively, including walking and biking around a local lake, day hikes, camping trips, backpack trips, and cross-country skiing. As Marcia, Marilynn, Diane, and Lynn each became financially independent following the nine-step program, they were treated to a monthlong trip in the UV to the desert Southwest. Most of the family would go along, with two or three at home as skeleton crew.

My backpacking trips with Vicki were highlights for me. We would have paper and pencil in hand as we walked, contemplating some creative topic we wanted to address. By the end of our trip, we'd have generated a mind map diagramming all the aspects we came up with to address the subject at hand. One time it was "Questions to consider if you are thinking of having a baby;" this resulted in a handout we called The Baby Questionnaire. Another time, the theme was "How to stay high in the city." We would refer to this once we were back in the thick of our work to tap into our higher selves and our aspirations.

Chapter 11

Emergent Properties

As we lived our principles to the best of our abilities, emergent properties arose from our group that were bigger than any one person: the heartbeat, of course, and also synergy, the group field, and our group DNA. The heartbeat was the essence or underlying spirit, the inherent glow, of this group of people. It was the rhythm that occurred when we were together and embodying our visions, principles, and values. Synergy was what happened in the outer world when our heartbeat was strong. The group field was what it looked and felt like to others. Our group DNA was what we each took out into the world with us—a personalized version of our heartbeat.

The Heartbeat

You could look at the ten of us and wonder what was going on with each person individually. We certainly each had our own experience of these years together, our own individual thread. But there was also a collective heartbeat that was bigger than any one of us. It was the result of embodying our foundational principles. Everything we did and how we acted came from our spiritual foundation, our commitment to spiritual growth, and our connection to vision and purpose. These all shaped who we were.

My journal from the well-oiled machine days tells of my struggles to live up to my ideals, to live from love as best I could, and it also tells of the immense satisfaction of what we shared and experienced together. Every so often, I'd ask myself if I still wanted to be there, and no matter whether I was in a hard place in my life or happy, the answer was always, "Yes, this is the best game in town. There's nowhere else I'd rather be." And it did feel like a game: how to be the most loving I can be, bring out the best qualities in me, and offer them to the group and be the wisest I could be. I felt privileged to be a part of this undertaking. And the big reason why I stayed was the heartbeat—the energy that I was being bathed in and that I now miss so much.

When I met the UV Family at Dinosaur National Monument, for the first time in my life, I felt seen and valued for who I was beyond the nerdy scientist. They saw the yearning for something more, for meaning in my life. They saw the untapped love in a soft but untrained and inexperienced heart. I felt accepted and loved for the totality of my being as it was right then, in all its naivete and innocence. After I had started living with the family, I had another precious experience I hadn't felt before: being cherished. Sure, my parents cherished me, but somehow, that wasn't conveyed to me in a way I could experience it. To be seen and cherished for who I was and their delight that I was in their life—such precious gifts. And to continuously experience that and from many other people was precious beyond measure. This allowed me to step into my Divine self.

I thrived on the intimacy we shared on a daily basis, from our nude morning gatherings to random hugs to a loving glance to a moment of laughter or of deep understanding. I listened to others and experienced the gift of being listened to deeply, of being heard. Others helped me through hard times, and I helped others. I felt a reassuring sense of security and safety, knowing others respected me and were committed to me.

This deep rootedness in mutual love, intimacy, respect, and security provided a platform from which each of us could soar, according to our own gifts and inclinations. We could lead, we could follow—it didn't matter. We were all creating together. And we knew we weren't doing it alone. We were constantly being inspired and uplifted by each person's individual expression of their divinity. We had enthusiasm for life, for one another, for our work, for ideas, and for other people and other projects.

If I faltered in enthusiasm and wanted a lift, I could find joy or laughter or at least curiosity and caring about my plight somewhere in that house. If I wanted to share a joy or a personal revelation or a new idea for our work, someone would want to hear it and share in my enthusiasm. If I was exuberant about something I had just read, others gladly listened to my excitement. If it was unrealistic, they might gently bring me back to earth, but more often than not, my excitement would feed them. If I was dragging from spending too much time doing data analysis in our computer closet, someone would give me a back rub or take me for a walk. I didn't have to go far to be uplifted or inspired. And I could provide that for others.

There was an underlying focus and harmony to our lives. Witness the *kitchen dance*. Our kitchen was not designed for a group our size. When someone was at the stove, you couldn't open the dishwasher. And if you were at the refrigerator, you could get trapped there by someone loading the dishwasher or taking something out of the oven. But we learned to dance around one another, intuitively coordinating our movements to allow six of us to be cooking or cleaning up from a big meal, with each person operating in a tight sphere but moving the whole process along. It was like a choreographed dance, where each knew their part and remained constantly aware of everyone else so that their movements fit in with the flow. Even years later when we gathered for a reunion, in an unfamiliar kitchen that was equally poorly designed, we still knew how to do this dance.

This was the heartbeat we were bathed in.

Synergy
Of course, we "danced" and collaborated in our work too, leading to the emergent property of synergy.

To keep us all going in the same direction required close communication and constant tacking (honing, course correction), sometimes ever so slightly. It might be a shift in the tone of our message, or realizing that connecting with a particular person was key to staying on course, or restating or revising the vision, or voicing the next steps to take. Our ultimate goal was listening to Lola. Out of such open-hearted connection, aligned for a purpose greater than self, we encountered synergy, an effect greater than the sum of our individual efforts. This is what made the well-oiled machine hum.

Joe used an image from ice skating called "crack the whip," to describe synergy. A line of skaters would join hands and gather speed. Then the leader would jerk the next person, who passed the jerk down the line to the end. The last person would be flung forward with great speed, circling around to become the new leader. His increased momentum would pull everyone along even faster. As this process was repeated, the speed got faster and faster.

It was a metaphor for the way we operated—leadership shifting from one person to another, depending on who was being flung forward. The leader boosted the rest of us to bring us *all* to a new level. The leader was supported by the others, and none could create this level of activity without all the others in the line. A truly synergistic effort. This happened not just in our work but also in our spiritual lives. One person's insight could bring us all to a higher level of awareness, and someone else would be propelled with yet another insight, bringing us along with them.

When we were operating at our finest, we experienced something similar to what George Yeoman Pocock in *The Boys in the Boat* called *swing*, where bodies, minds, and hearts are operating as one. When swing happened with the rowing crew, the boat was propelled at a smooth and fast rate that seemed almost effortless. They were all rowing together, synchronized, doing their best, looking out for one another.

Joe once commented, "If anyone falls out of sync with the synergistic whole, you can hear the grinding of the machinery like sand dumped into the gears." Vicki saw it this way: "If you have egos in ten different flavors and no higher purpose, they conflict. If you have ten different personality styles in synergy, then all the strengths come forward."

I relished being part of a team where other people did the jobs I didn't have the talent for or found impossible while I could concentrate on what I could offer. I was reassured knowing that Joe was keeping his eye on the big picture while each of us was doing our part. He could detect if our forward movement was imbalanced or moving astray, allowing us to course correct and return to synergizing quicker.

At a time when Evy and I were working hard on the ALS paper and everyone else was working hard on the FI book, and we were helping close friends of ours move, Joe equated the smooth functioning of the household to a good circuit:

> A good circuit gives off only a small amount of heat and has little harmonic distortion, qualities of our interactions lately. The ALS study and the FI book project are going along on parallel tracks as if they are in competition with each other even though they're not. There is probably a synergistic effect happening between them. A good circuit is also efficient (that is, frugal), which also fits for us—at many levels!

Once you experience this, you want more, and you become even more deeply bonded to your fellow synergists. This was our well-oiled machine. Like the swing of the rowing team, or the feeling of oneness in a jazz improv group, or the flow of a conversation that results in new possibilities, these times felt like a grace, a celestial symphony. The more well-oiled the machine, the more lyrical the symphony, the louder the heartbeat.

Quantum physicist David Bohm (as cited in Jaworski 1996) observed:

> At present, people create barriers between each other by their fragmentary thought. Each one operates separately. When these barriers have dissolved, then there arises one mind, where they are all one unit, but each person also retains his or her own individual awareness. That one mind will still exist even when they separate, and when they come together, it will be as if they hadn't separated. It's actually a single intelligence that works with people who are moving in relationship with one another. Cues that pass from one to the other are being picked up with the same awareness, just as we pick up cues in riding bicycles

or skiing. Therefore, these people are really all one. The separation between them is not blocking. They are all pulling together. If you had a number of people who really pulled together and worked together in this way, it would be remarkable. They would stand out so much that everyone would know they were different.[5]

The Group Energy Field

Just as synergy is more than the sum of the parts, a group energy field—an invisible structure, like gravity, that exerts influence—can emerge that is also more than the sum of the individual members of the group. John Fetzer of the Fetzer Institute described this as the community itself becoming the center of creative consciousness rather than the individuals. Guests often experienced our group field when they entered our house or spent time with us. They didn't call it a group field, but it was clear that it wasn't just the individual people they were responding to, but something that was generated among us that was solid, nurturing, and supportive.

Thousands of intentional communities formed in the 1960s and 1970s, so in that our origin was not unique. It was a time of disillusionment with the status quo and of great experimentation. Each community had its own personality and group field. The unique field that was created as we tried to embody our principles looked something like this, according to what guests, friends, and colleagues have told us:

- People living their beliefs.
- People who had heard the call and were acting on it.
- Realness. We were being ourselves.
- People living the spiritual ideals that others had read about.
- People who were 100 percent present.
- The quality of our relationship with one another—the harmony, integrity, honesty, love, and happiness.
- The quality of "being" we had.

[5]Jaworski, Joseph. *Synchronicity: The Inner Path of Leadership* (San Francisco, Calif.: Berrett-Koehler Publishers, 1996), 81

- Our openness to the new person.
- A place to experience growth, verify it, and get feedback.
- The experience of being totally accepted or unconditionally loved.
- The experience of being nurtured.
- The experience of sitting in a room not dominated by people full of ego.
- Our quirkiness.

Our Group DNA

In a sense, during our years together, each one of us was constantly creating the whole. The whole would have been different without any one of us, but the whole was also within each of us. Our *group DNA*—that is, our values, principles, and ways of being and acting—were embedded in each person, part of our core identity. Encountering any one of us, you would have gotten a flavor of our heartbeat.

Late in the well-oiled machine years, as we were reflecting on our lives together, one after another of us noted that people we encountered outside our circle picked up on this DNA. As we went about our lives, each of us carried this essential spirit, this heartbeat, with us and expressed it in our own unique way wherever we were.

Part III

Transformation:
From Well-Oiled Machine
to Living System

Chapter 12

Joe's Illness and Death

A year after *Your Money or Your Life* was published in 1992, Joe was diagnosed with metastatic lymphoma. He would live with this cancer for three and a half years.

Joe chose to keep the cancer private because he didn't want to be treated as a condition, and in this society, so-called cancer victims are often treated that way. He wanted to continue with his work and for other people to continue their work, without the focus being on *his* cancer. He said that, like our sexual relationship, the public didn't need to know, that it distracted from our mission. So for those three and a half years, all ten of us took his illness step by step, but kept it to ourselves.

His spiritual life and beliefs were key to how he dealt with cancer and the prospect of dying. He gave the illness the energy it needed and no more. His spiritual practice was equanimity at every step of the way. "Ah, so" when things looked bad, "Ah, so" when things looked good. He was grateful for each day, focusing on his work and on others rather than on himself. He hated what he called the screaming me-me-me's when all his energy needed to be focused on himself and his body. He was as honest with his thoughts and feelings as he knew how to be. He would tell us when he felt down or discouraged, but it never lasted long. Equanimity, letting go, no expectations, other-centeredness, love, purposeful activity—all of these were important for him. A sense of humor was really important during this time too. He was always cracking jokes about his condition or we were.

One of the keys for him in this whole process was that he knew he had led a fulfilling life and that his life was complete. There was nothing more he *needed* to do before he died. Every day was gravy—a gift. He had lived life to the fullest. He was ready to die whenever his time came.

As for treatment, he opted for what would allow him to still have quality of life. He was quite willing at any time to say, "No more treatment," or "No more of this particular treatment." And, while his quality of life did vary, he maintained it at a level that worked for him.

One vignette sticks out in my mind. He and I were alone in the house when it was lunchtime. He wasn't feeling very well, and when I asked what he wanted for lunch, he asked for his favorite comfort food, cheese quesadillas, even though it wasn't a healthy choice for him. It was an intimate moment of him being vulnerable and me realizing the most loving thing I could do was give him what he wanted. When I brought him his plate of comfort food, he looked at me with grateful eyes.

Our Process with Joe's Illness and Dying

After the initial shock of Joe's diagnosis had diminished, the rest of us in the household—we women—realized we had homework to do. We had already started meeting as a women's circle before Joe was diagnosed to strengthen ourselves, to strengthen the bond among us women, and to access our own inner knowing without the influence of Joe's strong personality and maleness. Now that format became essential to exploring this new territory of "What if we lose Joe?"

We naturally depended on one another for many aspects of our lives together, both personal and work-related. Now it was time to examine how we depended on Joe. What did each of us need to do to let go of our particular form of dependence on him for advice, for affection, for vision, or for practical matters like fixing a computer or repairing the vacuum cleaner? And what did we as a group need to do to empower ourselves to handle the practical matters Joe handled and the particular ways he had become essential to our group process and well-being? What did we need to do, individually and collectively, to come to peace with his possible death?

The easiest part was listing the tasks he did around the house and for our nonprofit foundation, and we learned what we could from Joe about how to do those tasks. The harder part was how to embody the roles Joe played in our lives, as we would see later.

When Joe was diagnosed, I knew that I had inner work to do. I hadn't had much experience being around someone who was dying or losing someone really close to me. I wanted to find a way to demystify the whole process of dying and death. Vicki was in a similar situation, and the two of us gathered up our courage and enrolled in a hospice training for volunteers. Then we each volunteered at a local, in-hospital hospice unit, learning the nitty-gritty of caring for the dying and getting more comfortable being around those who were close to death. This was not easy for me, but I was incredibly grateful to have both the training and the hands-on experience. This ran the gamut from changing the bedpan of a dignified music teacher with colon cancer, to scaring up a special food requested by another patient, to sitting with a woman who was in between worlds, reaching out over and over again for something or someone unseen. I felt much better prepared for whatever might happen with Joe or wherever death might show up next in my life.

Keeping Joe's cancer a secret was painful for me. I understood his rationale, and I respected his wishes. But I felt like I couldn't be honest even with our closest friends outside the immediate family about the most important thing that was going on in my life. This caused me much inner distress; and I puzzle to this day about how I could have responded differently or if there had been a way for Joe to share openly about his cancer and have it be a teaching opportunity rather than taking away from his work. Could he have accepted that he had a role to play in demystifying the big C?

Over the years of Joe's illness, we had many discussions about death. I had been formulating my own theories about what happened to a soul after death, and I asked him if he believed in any kind of life after death. His response was, "No. When you're dead, you're dead-dead." So right then and there, I asked him, "If you die before me, will you find a way to give me a sign if you aren't dead-dead?" He said yes. This exchange was really important to me because if I knew there was some part of him, like his soul, that had survived death, that would be immensely reassuring and would also help me in my own beliefs about death. I was grateful I had asked him that.

Joe's Last Days and Death

In December 1996, Joe opted for no more chemo so that he would qualify for an experimental drug trial using monoclonal antibodies in early January. We were beginning to allow ourselves to entertain the possibility of remission or even of a cure if he could get into the study. But by late December, his cancer had transformed into a virulent form, untreatable except by massive chemo that would only stave off the inevitable by a few months. And thus, he was no longer eligible for the experimental study.

While he was in the hospital learning the bad news, we had our hands full at home after two feet of snow fell, followed by heavy rain. This caused major flooding in our basement, and most of us were outside in the dark with shovels digging a channel to divert the water from the house. For me, at least, my nose was wet not just from dripping rain but from tears of grief. It seemed like everything was weeping. Then we had to scramble to keep supplies we had stored in the basement out of the water and to rig up a system to pump the water out. In addition, the heavy, wet snow had to be shoveled off the carport roof—a back-breaking job. Meanwhile, during the snowstorm, our family doctor, holding out his stethoscope instead of his thumb, hitchhiked to the hospital to lend his compassionate support and guidance to Joe. When we all met at the hospital later to hear the news, he met us at the entrance and ushered us up to Joe's room, embracing us in his caring.

Joe's quality of life deteriorated during this time, and by New Year's Day when he came home from the hospital, he and we knew he had only a matter of weeks left. We hunkered down, with minimal interactions with the outside world, doing our work and tending to Joe and to ourselves as best we could. During this time, I think we were each hoping and maybe expecting that we'd have some intimate, last words with Joe, where we could say goodbye or give and receive some token or message of love and caring. But that's not where Joe's focus was, and he evidently felt that everything had already been said. So the most we received were hints and tips on how to do practical things. Our daily reminder to ourselves was, "With nothing of myself in the way."

Two days before he died, he composed this announcement: "Joe Dominguez has been given a clean bill of death (date to be determined). Please direct your attention to the living and to the things that need to be done." He may not have realized his death would be quite so soon, and he wanted us and everyone else who by then knew he was dying to not get swept up by his dying and death, but to keep focused on what was important. Not to let an opportunity for gallows humor go by, he added a note to the card, "PS: It was not the salmon mousse." This was a reference to a Monty Python skit where the grim reaper, when asked how someone had died, pointed his bony finger at the salmon mousse they had just eaten.

His message was hard for me to take in and to follow. I was already deeply grieving his upcoming death, and his plea for us to focus on doing the things that needed to be done set a tone and focus where there was no room for my grief and feelings. Joe didn't want to be around a bunch of weeping women, and I had to find a way to respect that need and not burden him with my sadness. Later, these pent-up feelings would make my grief process a long and emotional one.

That same day, after working out some medication with the hospice nurse that would allow him a span of alert, focused time, he had a full work day. This was wonderful for him. It was important for him to leave us as well-prepared as possible to deal with the practical matters of running NRM and our household.

When it was clear that Joe was in the throes of dying, we all gathered near his bed and chanted his favorite chant, the great mantra of the Buddhist Heart Sutra, "Gate gate paragate parasamgate bodhi svaha"—"Gone, gone, gone beyond, gone altogether beyond, O what an awakening, all hail!" At one point, he lifted his finger up, following along with the chant, and then he was gone. We gathered around him, saying our farewells, our blessings and thank-yous. Then all nine of us washed his body. When we were ready, we called the funeral home—and thus began our life without Joe in it.

We have a photo of us in the front yard the day after Joe died, with the pale, winter sun on our wan, drawn faces. A whole new chapter in our lives was beginning, and it was all uncharted territory. With Joe's death, we had lost our primary lover and source of male energy. And we had lost a lot more. His leadership and long-range thinking had kept us on track, and he had been our most reliable frequency for tuning in to Lola. He had spoken from inner authority. He could see through to the core of an issue, and his contrarian thinking had allowed him to think outside the box and solve problems in surprising ways. His visionary capacity had pointed us to the highest ground on which we could stand. He had been our information hub and the glue that held us together. He had kept tabs on our comings and goings, our group dynamics, our work, and the world situation. He had been our protector, and we had known he had always had our backs—ready to come to our aid, whether physically or when we were doing something out of our comfort zone for our work. With his natural feistiness, he had been willing to say or do what needed to be done without concern for what others thought of him. He had also been a source of spiritual wisdom and nurturing, and he could take a situation and transform it into humor or a teaching story. And we would soon come to keenly miss his ability to fix things in our house, as you'll see shortly.

Something that buoyed our spirits during this time was the daily outpouring of heartfelt faxes, emails, and letters from friends, colleagues, and people who knew Joe through our financial work, describing what Joe meant to them and their understanding of the magnitude of loss this was for us. Sister Miriam MacGillis, a colleague and friend from Genesis Farm, an ecological center in New Jersey, referred to Joe's "infectious laugh, his brilliant capacity to cut through the crap and redeem the heart of the matter." Donella Meadows, another colleague and friend and lead author of the book *The Limits to Growth: A Report for the Club of Rome's Project on the Predicament of Mankind*, wrote, "By the very nature of his aliveness and determination and humor and sense of mission, he leaves behind a huge emptiness." She referred to him as the "full, mischievous, opinionated, warm, and original Joe."

My Process

A powerful understanding for me right after Joe died was the realization that Thy (i.e., God's) will had been done! I had prayed and prayed beforehand for Thy will to be done, and Joe had kept getting worse and worse. When he died, I got like I'd never gotten before that Thy will had been done; *my* will was that Joe live, but clearly, God's will was that Joe die—so many doors kept closing on him from the beginning. So with that recognition, acceptance of "what is" was easier because it was clearly in the grand scheme of things for Joe to die now.

Even with the acceptance, my heart broke open in grief. I had lost my primary lover, a partner in the work, a source of inspiration and vision, and my spiritual teacher. I lost the person in my life who I felt had loved me most unconditionally, who had always had faith in me, who had always seen the best in me, who had been there when I got stuck or needed advice, who had helped me begin to love my whole self, including my body. He had instilled in me a sense of security and self-worth. I knew I had been loved and cherished by him. There were aspects of his personality that I certainly wouldn't miss, but these were overshadowed by the sense of loss.

We hadn't divulged our group marriage to the general public out of our desire to appear respectable so that our relationship wouldn't undermine our work and our credibility. Joe and Vicki, as coauthors of *Your Money or Your Life*, were thought to be a couple, and we had done nothing to disabuse that. So when Joe died, people thought just Vicki had lost her husband. Only a few people knew that I had also lost *my* husband—my primary male relationship—and could understand the extent of my grief.

While we were all spiritual teachers for one another, Joe held a special place in my spiritual life. He had been the Rock of Gibraltar spiritually for me. He had had an enlightenment experience and then spent the rest of his life trying to live it. He by no means had been a saint, but he still had had wisdom that I wanted and had benefited from. He had related to the highest in each of us, even when we had lost touch with it ourselves.

After his death, I prayed for a teacher to enter my life to help me through this excruciating time. My prayer was answered, but not in the way I had expected. A year after Joe died, I began having vivid dreams of a whole different nature than I'd ever had. Many seemed to be teaching dreams, and I had to learn the language of dream symbols and metaphors. In many dreams, Joe was back from the dead, and in one special dream, he offered me a blessing. I have often wondered if this was Joe's way of letting me know he wasn't "dead-dead." I like to think so. Regardless, I am immensely grateful for the comfort of these dreams, even the nightmares, because I was able to use them to put one foot in front of the other and find my way through what seemed like a wasteland inside myself.

Perhaps what I missed the most was what *we* had lost. Joe had been integral to almost every decision, to articulating our vision, to our work, to our staying on track, and to reminding us of the grand opportunities we had to serve the world. He had been like the bright, contrasting color in a weaving that brings the whole cloth together into a stunning piece. In another sense, we had lost a part of our hologram. Fortunately, the beauty of a hologram is that the image and essence remain even when part of it is missing. Here's what I wrote at that time: "We are a hologram, so we've lost a little bit of resolution (i.e., definition), but all the pieces are still there. We become a little fuzzier than we were, but we still exist and Joeness still exists."

Hand in hand with missing Joe, grieving, and coming to accept Joe's death was fear of change, fear of the unknown, and resisting "what is." As time went on, I would be one of the ones holding on so tightly to the past that I couldn't see that this was not only unsustainable and impractical but contrary to what Spirit had in store for us. I simply couldn't believe we weren't supposed to stay together and continue with our work. In addition, and maybe more importantly, I simply had a very hard time embracing change. Of course, the only wise choice when clinging desperately to the past is to let go.

Chapter 13

Disintegration, Transformation, and Unraveling

It felt to me as if the hand of God had come down and taken Joe out of our system and disrupted our lives, sending us on a whole new journey whose map had not been revealed to us. My sense that Spirit was at work in this provided hope that we would find our way through this bewildering new state of affairs. I can look back now and map some of that transformative journey as seen and experienced through my eyes.

Grief, Chaos, and Letting Go

Within days of Joe's death, both Evy and Vicki had cut their hair short. Joe had liked long hair, and they had accommodated him, but now there was no longer a reason to keep their hair long unless they wanted to. To me, it seemed like a statement that "That was then, this is now. I'm moving on and claiming my right to change." And I was shocked that they would change the way things were so soon after his death. That's when I knew that I, at least, was in for a rough ride. For me, that's when the unraveling of our group began.

How often do nine women grieve the loss of the same lover? This involved nine individual grief processes, plus the grief process of our *group soul*. We reminded ourselves that we needed to give space for each of us to grieve in our own unique ways. And in fact, we grieved very differently. For some, handling practical details and keeping busy was important. For others, making phone calls to let people know of Joe's death was comforting. I was pretty useless, just managing to do the basics that needed to be done, like attending group meetings, helping with simple tasks like kitchen cleanup, and doing my own self-care.

Imagine the nine of us circled up after Joe died, looking around, and scratching our heads, asking ourselves, "What are nine mostly heterosexual women committed to one another supposed to be doing together?" Initially, most of us just assumed we would continue to live and work together, that the Grand Adventure would go on. After all, Joe had said before he had died, "If you all disband after I die, my life will have been in vain." We wondered if maybe we had some mission that we didn't even know yet, but that we were somehow meant to be a group of ever more powerful women, living and working together in love. Perhaps our work was to act as a voice for feminine wisdom and its critical need in our world at this time. So we analyzed the roles that Joe had filled and how we could fill those without him.

But the chaos, which had begun before Joe had died with the snowstorm and flooding of the basement, just got worse. Our vacuum cleaner, dishwasher, and microwave all broke; the basement was still flooding; and our hot water heater began to leak, further flooding the basement. And of course there was our inner chaos—individually and collectively. I took heart from an article by Michael R. Butz saying that chaos indicates that we have lived in one state of order long enough. Joe's death shattered our order, forcing us to evolve. Okay, so now what?

At one point, I called Sister Miriam MacGillis, who had been an occasional guide through this process. Her first question was, "Is the shit hitting the fan yet?" How did she know?! In essence, she said the following:

> Joe was able to pull something out of you bigger than the group. When such a charismatic presence is removed, there must be chaos. You're forced to look at "Who are we without Joe?" It's part of the process of transformation, and if you weren't going through it, something would be wrong.

This is the time for faith. Times like this strip away assurances and guarantees, and all you have to rely on is faith. Faith is putting one foot in front of the other when you don't know what's underneath. And having faith in the people you throw your lot with and faith in the vision you're called to. You can't get a new vision until you're stripped of everything. You have to be in the desert now, but it always leads to another, deeper threshold. God is in the whole thing; you're going to be all right.

So we began to accept that without Joe's magnetism, life would never be the same. As Vicki said, "One way you could construe it is, 'Oh God, things are falling apart.' Or another way you could construe it is, 'Life is bursting through this system.'"

Letting go was an ongoing process that each of us had to experience in our own way. We also had to let go of some of our ideals, of the story we told about our lives together as a well-oiled machine, of our tight control over NRM and our work, of our attachment to certain material possessions, and of our attachment to one another. We had to evaluate and decide what to keep from the past, both materially and otherwise. And we had to find ways to liberate one another.

This whole process forced us to plumb our spiritual depths and our inner lives. We wanted to bring more sacredness into our daily lives, and over time, many of us were drawn to deeper explorations of our spirituality. Individual and group transformation was all happening simultaneously, even as we tried to keep our nonprofit foundation running and our work moving forward.

For me, my inner exploration took precedence over our work. I found that on joining this family, I had surrendered my sense of self before I really had one, and I realized that developing this self was paramount. In contrast, moving our work forward was essential for Vicki's process, and she felt frustrated and disappointed when some of us simply couldn't join her there. When we had a little more perspective about what was going on, we described it as Vicki valiantly shaking the apple trees, but precious little fruit would fall for all her efforts to get us on board.

Two months after Joe died, all nine of us took a monthlong trip in the UV to the Anza-Borrego Desert State Park in southern California. In the early days of the UV Family, this desert had been a favorite place to camp for extended periods of time for deep personal and group nourishment. It became a spiritual home for them, and as those of us who joined later visited this desert, it became our spiritual home too. We have invested the Yaqui Well area and a particular ironwood grove with a lot of love. Marshal South describes the area perfectly:

> *A few steps down the dry dirt road and the desert wraps you around with its friendly blanket. You are as much in the solitude of the waste-lands as though you were a thousand leagues from modern Progress. Smoke trees stalk like grey ghosts down the harsh gravel of the bush-grown wash. And creosote bushes and burroweed compete for place with the bristling heads of the Bigelow chollas. Ocotillos writhe their spiny wands toward the sun and cast a basket-work of ragged shad-ows from which little groups of drowsing quail scurry off, startled, at advancing footsteps. It is very quiet. And over all brood the mountain ridges. The ironwood trees are inviting havens of shade against the sere glare of the sun-scorched slopes.*[6]

Our trip was a huge undertaking in many ways. It was the first time the UV had gone on a trip without Joe as driver and the first time we had all been on a trip together. We were still actively grieving and vulnerable. But we all agreed that we needed to be in our spiritual home in the desert and leave Joe's ashes there. Fortunately, many people stepped forward to handle NRM business while we were gone, and Evy's parents even traveled from Nebraska to be part of the home team. As we piled into the UV and the two cars that would be accompanying it, someone said into the CB radio, "Ladies, start your engines," and somehow, that captured the spirit that we intended to bring to this time. It communicated the gutsy nature of this trip and the whole grieving journey—saying yes to life even in the midst of grief.

---

[6]South, Marshal. *Marshal South and the Ghost Mountain Chronicles: An Experiment in Primitive Living* (San Diego, Calif.: Sunbelt Publications, 2005), 270.

Once we arrived, we began calling ourselves the Desert Mamas. This was a pivotal time for us in many ways. Each of us had time and space to grieve in our own ways. We spent many hours with the nine of us circled up amid the ironwood trees and creosote bushes bringing more self-awareness to who we were becoming as a group. Every evening after dark, the Hale-Bopp comet hovered on the horizon, and it felt like a blessing on our endeavor.

"Mystery," from *Missa Gaia/Earth Mass* by Paul Winter became my theme song as I walked up and down a remote sandy wash during my retreat time in the desert. Reaching out to mystery and surrendering to the mystery of this time of grief, bewilderment, and upheaval gave me something to hang on to, something to put my faith and trust in.

During this retreat, I realized that the most powerful way to move forward without Joe was to embody some of the things I missed most about him. I vowed to be more available to others and bring more loving kindness to my interactions with others. I also vowed to be a voice for synergy and finding ways to nurture our expressions of intimacy during this time of transition.

The desert worked its magic on us, and we returned to Seattle feeling more solid and clear in ourselves and as a group.

Conflict and Emotions

The months right after Joe's death were characterized by more interpersonal and group conflict than we would have thought possible, starting with designing Joe's memorial service. Our lack of clarity about how to hold and work with emotions made conflict resolution even harder.

Mercifully, Marcia proposed that we all take a workshop in Seattle on nonviolent communication (also called compassionate communication) with Marshall Rosenberg, a peacemaker and founder of the Center for Nonviolent Communication. The workshop focused on how to responsibly communicate about difficult emotions. We all attended, and it was a turning point in our conflict. It gave us a tool for examining our own feelings and needs, taking responsibility for them, and being able to communicate in a more loving way with others.

And those of us who judged ourselves for having feelings learned to embrace, accept, and work through them with compassion for ourselves. Compassionate communication played an essential role in our lives from that point on. And we wished we had had this tool while Joe had still been alive.

Leadership and Decision-making

Joe As Leader

For all the years we were together, we had resisted the notion that Joe was our leader. After all, he may have been the only male, but we were all powerful females in our own right. How could we let him get away with that? We were all doing this together, weren't we?

But he was charismatic, had a magnetic personality, was one of our best spokespeople, and was very wise. He could also articulate what was taking shape for us, the tapestry we were weaving, what we were beginning to live into but couldn't put into words, when the rest of us were too immersed in the process to see the bigger picture. So, he inspired us with his vision. These were all attributes of a good leader, no matter the gender, and all good reasons to bow to his wisdom. He had earned his authority.

In hindsight, after his death, and as our group began to unravel, we began to admit to ourselves and others, "Well, maybe he really was our leader." As Vicki says about his magnetism, "Around Joe, the iron filings lined up—they just did. And it was an is-ness."

The concept articulated by Werner Erhard of *power source* and *power feeder* was helpful to me as I tried to accept that in some sense Joe was the leader. In a group like ours, having both a power source and power feeders created an engine for getting things done in the world, for moving our ideas and message out into the world. Joe ended up being our power source, and we were all power feeders. As long as we were totally focused on our mutually shared dream and weren't being unduly influenced by our egos, this dynamic worked, and we all benefited.

The dynamic tension of this power source/power feeder relationship depended on each of us drawing deep inside to be our most individuated, unique, powerful selves. At its best, this created the well-oiled machine, and we basked in the synergy that resulted. If any of us flagged in holding the vision or in our ability to respond from our highest selves (as sometimes happened), or if Joe overstepped his authority as power source (as he sometimes did), then we felt constrained or dominated by him and there was less energy and clarity going out into the world.

Vicki concluded later:

> *Joe's role as power source was a vital part of what made this visionary group successful. So you have to talk about Joe and his power in the group if you want to describe what made us tick. We were drawn by Joe and by the dream—both/and. We were all together for the dream as well as for our particular attraction to Joe, but the dream couldn't have resulted in the masterpiece without the power source Joe provided. No wonder we gradually broke up after Joe died. He was the center of our Universe, in a positive way.*

It took reading *Charisma and Social Structure: A Study of Love and Power, Wholeness and Transformation* by Raymond Trevor Bradley for me to finally feel okay about Joe being the leader. Bradley studied communes and what made them successful or not. He discovered that a strong *hierarchy of power* (top down) combined with a strong *heterarchy of communion* (horizontal connections of love) produced the most successful long-term communes. Ours had fit this to a T. Joe had been at the top of the hierarchy, with Vicki next, followed by Evy and Monica. The heterarchy had resulted from the strong bonding among individuals within the family. Intentionally nurturing our one-on-one relationships with one another had been integral to forming and maintaining this heterarchy. Both the hierarchy and the heterarchy had been essential to our success. And when Joe had died, we had lost our leader and an integral part of what had made our family system work so well. Vicki had tried to step into the leadership role, but we couldn't conjure up the same willingness to follow as we had for Joe.

So was Joe the leader? In the hierarchy, yes; in the heterarchy, no. Now with him no longer our leader, we had to resist the trap of "How would Joe have done it?" or "What would Joe say?," and for the most part, we did.

New Leadership and Decision-making

During this time, when we needed to make decisions, we discovered new methods of tuning in to Lola using feminine wisdom:

- Circle wisdom. While we didn't trust any one of us to have the right answer, we did trust the group's wisdom.
- Turning more toward inductive rather than deductive reasoning, which meant following our hearts, faith, intuition, gut feelings, and love more than logic.
- Paying attention to attractions and aversions as possible messages from the Universe rather than just our egos speaking.
- Moments of silence for integration, regaining our centers, and creating space for new perspectives and insights.
- Trusting in the mysterious unfolding of life. Taking one step at a time and then assessing instead of having a grand plan.
- Reminding ourselves that all of us needed to be leaderful and that each person needed to be able to speak for herself.
- Listening to myriad sources of guidance, including friends, prophetic voices, "the call" (an inner prompting by Spirit toward a particular course of action), one another, Lola, events in the world, inner wisdom, and the Earth.
- Messages from our nighttime dreams. For example, one time I shared a dream that seemed to be for all of us about a beached whale. Vicki identified with the whale, and that realization allowed her and the group to move forward in a slightly new way. Sometimes the imagery from a dream helped us move out of our rational minds or added breadth and hope to our group process.

Truth-telling

We started having what we called *Us days* where we spent the whole day together discussing practical matters, our outer work, our inner lives, how to nourish our group soul, and where we were going as a group. Early on, as the parts of ourselves we had set aside for this Grand Adventure began to clamor for expression, the things that had been unhealthy or painful in our lives together began to reveal themselves in truth-telling sessions.

Shining the light of truth on our beliefs, behaviors, and actions was really hard for me to experience, and I am squirming as I write about it. We may have been aspiring saints, but we had our human failings, our clay feet, just like so many spiritual groups, and I'm afraid that my telling you our particular version of this will discredit all that we did and our work in your eyes. I'm afraid you will become disillusioned. You may be thinking, "Yet another spiritual group that doesn't live up to their precepts." I'm afraid you will put this book down in disgust and disregard the picture that I've painted up until now.

It's doubly hard to tell you about our dysfunctional behavior and shadow (our dark side, mostly unconscious) because we (or I, in my naivete, at least) thought we had tools and commitments in place to avoid having a large shadow. After all, we were committed to total honesty. It's probably a rare community that doesn't have a shadow, especially after twenty-five years, but we certainly intended to be an exception. Even before Joe died, though, we might have seen signs and symptoms had we stopped long enough and had the courage to address them. It took the earthquake of Joe's death to jolt us into seeing our shadow and start the process of truth-telling—an essential part of our healing and moving forward.

I found myself shocked, dismayed, disappointed, and disillusioned after what I learned in many of these sessions. It was excruciating for me to hear the ways one of us, or maybe even many of us, had sold out our power, not told the truth, withheld important experiences or emotions from the group, pretended to be on board when we weren't, or disavowed us as family or group marriage.

It blew my perception of who I thought we were. I had wanted our life together and our Grand Adventure to work so badly! And I have tenderness for the fact that we had all tried and awe at the privilege of being part of that grand effort. For my part, I truly did try to live our ideal, but I was complicit in the shadow too. My naive idealism sometimes blinded me to reality, and I can see that I was sometimes dishonest with and not true to myself. So I've had to accept that alongside the jewel that we were together, we had our human failings.

As our truth-telling sessions progressed, various themes emerged that helped us see some of the reasons we stumbled: rigidity of our so-called teachings and our organization, dishonesty, blind idealism, ignoring undercurrents of discontent, and selling out our power to Joe.

Rigidity, Dishonesty, Misguided Idealism

We began to see how rigid we had become, both as a family and as an organization. Monica and Vicki can trace the start of this inflexibility to the early 1980s when they began a more outer-focused, we-can-change-the-world life. They began to objectify their learnings into a teaching so it could be shared more easily with others. That led to trying to live up to an image and the tenets they were propounding instead of being constantly open to new discoveries and experiences. They had lost track of the humility of not knowing and the quest to live the truth as it presented itself moment by moment.

At the same time, they stopped their nightly practice of CS&T (Heart Sharing while high on pot) to allow time for more focused action. That meant they abandoned the daily practice of surrender that had helped them stay true to Spirit and themselves for the preceding ten years. When they began doing Heart Sharing without the support of the dope, it became easier to be less honest with themselves, and more ego crept in to muddy the insights and gifts of this sacred space that was so critical to being in their higher selves. By the time we were living in the Seattle house and Heart Sharing just once a week, the deepest levels of honesty and transparency were harder to access in ourselves and to admit. Somehow, it became less safe to be brutally honest. Over time, as we became more focused on our work, our Heart Sharings were sometimes rote, not accessing or revealing deeper issues and important understandings and insights.

As we marched passionately toward our heartfelt goals and promoted our body of teachings, a certain blindness and tunnel vision crept in. We were trying to uphold and live up to a big ideal, and the light of this vision blinded us. We presented this ideal to the world and were either blind to our human failings, hid them, or at least didn't give them much weight. To some extent, we weren't even able to talk about them among ourselves with total honesty.

Some friends and visitors found our intensity and focus overbearing and inauthentic. Maybe too virtuous. Later we would learn that some guests were greatly relieved when one of us would reveal a human shortcoming or issue. Others reflected back to us that what they really missed from us was more authenticity, more realness. They wanted us to model how to stay true to one's ideals while recognizing and accepting one's humanity, not separate from it or in denial of it.

Sometimes clinging to our ideals led to an ill-conceived audacity, self-righteousness, or even cold-heartedness. We learned too late that one couple who had been dear friends and colleagues felt abandoned by us at the time of their greatest need. Our zeal could come across as holier than thou, as if we were saying, "We know what's best for you." We sometimes judged behaviors we thought didn't fit our ideals, and there were times that I now regret where I didn't care enough about someone else's plight. The irony is that some behaviors I judged or scoffed at in those days have come back to haunt me as I've found myself doing those very things, like paying to exercise in a gym instead of depending on daily activities to stay in shape.

Also, in an attempt to hold on to our ideals, we withheld certain information from the general public. As I explained earlier, there were good reasons for this (for example, Joe's cancer, our group marriage), but it led to even less genuineness. It was easier to hide behind our beliefs and ideals than to show the public our human side, but doing so took its toll.

Ignoring the Seeds of Discontent

Looking back now, I can see that the seeds of our unraveling as a community had been sown long before Joe died. As Vicki said, "There were undercurrents that would have been our undoing had Joe not died."

For several years before his death, I had a major health problem that affected my stamina and ability to participate fully in our work.

Once I felt better, I began questioning what my role should be. I no longer felt as fulfilled or enlivened with what I was doing. At the same time, Evy was hearing an inner call to the ministry, but she didn't want to disturb the status quo while Joe was ill. Vicki was experiencing deep depressions. Marcia hadn't been thriving and left to volunteer for other organizations for months at a time. Monica had been doing her volunteer work in prisons for many years, with almost no support from our community, including me. Now, during this truth-telling time, we could see how cruel it was to not support her in her heart's calling.

The tendency to rigidify became even stronger as we became more embedded in the framework of a foundation that had to meet certain legal standards. We couldn't be as agile, unencumbered, and flexible as the UV Family had been. Vicki could look back and see that NRM had become a burden for the family long before Joe died—the work in some ways overwhelming the capacity of the people to do it and to stay connected.

Vicki recalls: "The mechanics of running an organization had begun to overshadow the fun parts, and it became burdensome. Eventually, our fixation on book sales in the years after *Your Money or Your Life* was published showed how *off* we had gotten."

Unwittingly and shockingly, we had lost sight of our prime directive to be what Vicki called "a generator of love." Instead, we had begun draining the pot of love to do "the work." We had become deeply involved in *doing* and lost some of our *being*—the *quality* of how things were done. We lost some of the heart of who we were, some of our heartbeat.

Selling Out Our Power to Joe

As we began to gain more clarity about our lives with Joe, we had to admit that we had often sold out our power to him. We had always held to the belief that we were ten powerful people. Nine of us were women and one was a man, but we each stood solid and empowered in ourselves. While that was true a lot of the time, the subtle dynamic of deferring to Joe as a man and an authority figure proved to be stronger than any of us had realized. In part, this reflected traditional gender roles in the culture we had grown up in. But we thought we had dismantled these roles or at least engaged in them consciously.

What I wrote in my diary years before Joe died reveals my ongoing ponderings on this subject:

> *When is deference appropriate? When any of us relates to Joe as the man or as an authority figure, we are relating to an object, not to the real person. When you react to gender or authority, you react with deference or with aggressiveness, either of which is swinging the pendulum from one end to the other. What we want to do is stand in Truth, which is at center. If Joe is at Truth and helps facilitate my arrival at Truth, that's great! Don't avoid Truth just because Joe is already standing there. Track record enters into the picture here because experience has shown us that, a large part of the time, Joe is standing in Truth. So when is it unhealthy deference, and when is it surrendering to Truth? One thing is to be willing to put out your own Truth and to be wrong some of the time, but to create your own track record.*

I certainly tried to do this, but I think my track record was uneven.

Of course, because Joe was a capable and wise leader in so many ways, it was difficult to recognize times when we were giving him unwarranted deference or allowing him to slip into abusing his authority. And because he was so influential in our group, any lapses really impacted us.

Through the years, many of us had become troubled by Joe's occasional outbursts of anger over seemingly small issues and demeaning language toward whomever he thought was at fault. At other times, his long-held judgment ended up keeping someone stuck in the very behavior he was belittling. He dismissed feelings and emotions as unnecessary and getting in the way of spiritual enlightenment. While to some extent that might have been true, on another more practical level, his blindness to the need for him to acknowledge and work with his own emotions led to increasing dysfunction. We learned to dissemble and keep our emotions more to ourselves, and this was unhealthy.

We tried various ways of talking with him about this in group, but he would accuse us women of ganging up on him. It took a real act of courage for any one of us to stand up to Joe. For one thing, his perspective often had validity. And it seemed that the others weren't willing to stand up for the woman who was sticking her neck out, so she would find herself out on the skinny branches all alone. Thus we learned not to do it very often or to do it with him in private.

The result was that we women had checks and balances on behaviors and attitudes that did not express the values we were trying to live—via reflections from one another and from Joe—but Joe had few consistent checks and balances on his. Consequently, he didn't grow out of them. This created a large dysfunction in our group that we did not see clearly enough until after he had died. Many of us feel that we did Joe and ourselves a huge disservice by not collectively and persistently calling him out on his failings, thereby helping him to continue evolving emotionally and spiritually.

Sometimes I did challenge Joe when I had a different perspective or confronted him on behavior that I thought was uncalled for. While he didn't necessarily acknowledge his failing, I would sometimes notice changes in how he acted afterward.

An area where we women have differing viewpoints even to this day is on Joe's sexual relationships with women outside of our group marriage. In a general sense, our family embraced inclusive relationships with other women and men whom one or another of us felt drawn to, as long as those involved took responsibility for the relationship and there was alignment with our shared values, openness and honesty, commitment, and a sense of appropriateness for all concerned. But did Joe carry that too far? Did he convince himself and us that the pyramid was right side up when it was actually upside down, led by sexual attraction and not a spiritual foundation with shared purpose?

There were several views among us nine women:

- Some of us held the viewpoint that this was the culture that had evolved in our family, and even though it might not have been to everyone's liking, we didn't intervene to change it.

- Others felt powerless to change this culture once it had been set in motion. They felt that Joe had an unhealthy need for sexual relationships with women, and some women may have been hurt by that.
- Still others thought that most of these relationships had been life-affirming and life-giving for those involved and that they had brought more love into the world.

I consider my sexual relationship with Joe and how it came about as a blessing and something I would not change. It felt healthy and clear from the very beginning. But the question remains, "How much was Joe operating from his highest self and for the highest good of other women outside the family?"

So Joe had his human frailties, and his impact on our lives was sometimes harm or belittlement or disempowerment. How could we women have allowed this dysfunction to persist? And why didn't we rebel or leave? The truth is that there was the dysfunction but there was also the diamond. None of us was willing to give up the vision by rocking the boat. No one wanted to risk losing the Grand Adventure. We loved one another, and we loved Joe—his generous spirit, his holding each of us as his beloved, his feistiness, his vision, his clarity, and his energy. His intention always was to make the world a better place, and he made immense contributions to that end. We stayed together for the love, the beauty, and the fulfillment that was there. But the vision couldn't be sustained without challenging the status quo.

Well, the boat got rocked for us when Joe died.

Were We a Cult?
You might be asking yourself, "Were they a cult?" I had asked myself that question occasionally over the years as a double-check on myself. The answer for me was always no. Certainly from the outside, we had some cultish behaviors. We had a charismatic leader. We often spoke as one voice, so people had a hard time getting to know us as individuals. And we had all the dysfunction I've just described.

But the bottom line for me was asking myself, "Am I acting or responding with cultish behavior? Do I feel stuck in this group? Or do I feel empowered?" To the degree that I felt trapped and powerless and let Joe run the show, I colluded with cultish behavior. But I always knew I had a choice. I could in any moment think for myself and be as powerful as I was willing and able to be. Because we kept our personal finances separate, I knew I could leave at any time. I was only tied to the group by love and the vision we carried.

Years later, Vicki says:

This is the story of my idealistic community—the story of trying to live the truth and basically developing a huge shadow that none of us could see. It's taken years to understand, with great compassion for myself, how I suppressed my basic human self in an effort to become the spiritual ideal that I thought was so possible. You can make that cultic consciousness wrong, or you can say we were very young and fumbling along, and that has brought us to a more textured and mature understanding.

You, the reader, will have to decide for yourself. For me, it was certainly not a cult.

Relationship to the Outside World

As we examined how we had allowed ourselves to get so off course, it became clear that we had become too insulated and not open to course correction from outside our group. So we breathed new life into our group through new community members and more enrichment from outside. We allowed and welcomed more flow-through of people and ideas in our life. We saw the importance of being fully real with our friends, being more vulnerable with them than we had in the past, and we adopted new and more human and authentic ways of being with others. We valued the input of our outside friends and partners as they reflected back to us who we were becoming, shared their own experiences, and reminded us to enjoy life.

I remember when Elisabet Sahtouris, an evolution biologist and futurist, visited us. She asked about each of us sitting around the table and where we were in our lives. When my turn came, I almost burst into tears as I said, "I don't know who I am!" Her response was, "Doing what brings us joy is what the world needs," and I experienced her full acceptance of me and where I was in my process. That allowed me to be less ashamed of my not knowing, and I felt a deep relief and trust that over time I would come to know who I was and where my joy was.

We learned that there is a tradeoff between *certainty* and *wholeness*: If you are certain of your vision and how to do it, then you aren't open to input and gifts from others that might lead to more wholeness. Joe was certain, and that certainty allowed him and us to produce a great body of work, but we sacrificed a wholeness. Now it seemed like we had less certainty, but we were beginning to experience more wholeness.

Inner Transformation and Individuation
Abandoning Parts of Ourselves
In all our years together, we experienced what the communal energy could do in the world, and that's why we lived in community. We had willingly sacrificed some of our sense of separate self for the collective, for the *we*. But the balance had tipped too far in favor of the we at the expense of our individual selves.

Vicki reflects on this:

> It was human beings doing all this work. And the human beings all set aside parts of themselves in order to enter into the Heroic Journey. And we did it willingly, gloriously. Nobody made us do it. And I think if Joe hadn't died, I would have done this until the day I died. No question. But once that magnet was out of the center, those parts of ourselves that had not had an opportunity to live in a while started to want to live.

Even the most beautiful world can become a prison! And ours eventually did. Marcia mused, "We so held to our vision and were so committed to that that we lost our individual freedom." We all had our unlived lives to claim.

For myself, I had experienced the rewards of self-negating for the good of the whole, but it wasn't until now that I became aware of the costs. Five years before Joe died, when I was struggling with my health, my doctor observed that what he saw in me, as well as other members of our household, was the physical manifestation of austerity or self-sacrifice. He said we were ripping ourselves off in the process of serving. At the time, I dismissed his warning, but now I remembered this and realized what he was talking about. I had a lot of sadness— both for the suppression of my basic human self and for the loss of the spiritual ideal we had been trying to live. I keenly felt the loss of the *we*, even as I knew I needed to cultivate my *me*.

Individuation/Differentiation

So without realizing exactly what we were doing, one by one, we began identifying and reclaiming these abandoned parts of ourselves that wanted to live, that wanted to be free. This process of individuation would be a hallmark of the rest of our time together.

We tried to liberate ourselves and our creative potentials without destroying the foundation, the heartbeat, the beauty. From time to time, someone would hear their own special calling, and we began to realize this was an important part of our process and that we needed to give one another space for these soul callings. Most of us began seeking wisdom and enrichment outside our circle in the form of workshops, retreats, spiritual groups, networking, and discussions with friends.

Some of us were being called more strongly to seek inner transformation and others to promoting social transformation, so there was a wide spectrum among us. Some of us seemed to be shifting from being activists to becoming wisdom keepers and sharers. We had to trust that this inner work was what the world needed from us at that time.

During this period, someone visiting us who was known for his courageous activism asked me what was alive for me. I shared my struggle of being in transition and not knowing what was next but being drawn to the inner realms. I felt embarrassed to admit this to a die-hard activist. But he pointed out that the inner life is not supported in this culture, so it's easy to question oneself on this. He said that there needs to be an integration of activism and inner life, an integration of doing and being. His understanding and perspective allowed me to be more accepting of this inner pull.

I was inspired to start a "Wolvies" group based on Clarissa Pinkola Estés's book *Women Who Run with the Wolves: Myths and Stories of the Wild Woman Archetype* after attending such a group when I was visiting Sister Miriam MacGillis at Genesis Farm. Many of our household joined in, as well as other friends. Discussing the book and doing exercises in it were important ingredients in my individuation process and reclaiming parts of myself that had been buried since childhood.

Of course, our individuation came at a price. There was a huge decrease in synergy in our work as people's energy became more focused on individual explorations and projects. This was a huge loss to me, even though my energy was also focused on my own explorations. Still, I kept hoping that we were synergizing in some new way I couldn't quite see.

In addition, we lost more and more of the group identity as we claimed our own identities. And we lost the tight-knit support we had come to expect in the well-oiled machine days. We simply couldn't muster that kind of energy anymore. We could no longer count on one another to be there for us in the way that we used to be. For example, those whose energies were being drawn elsewhere or who had moved out couldn't necessarily expect that those who continued living in the house and kept NRM afloat would have the time and energy to provide the same level of companionship, help, or shelter that had previously been our norm. For me, reciprocity was key—we couldn't take one another for granted.

Also, as we *Sisters* (how we started referring to us nine women— like a blending of close spiritual companions and close siblings) began to individuate, we simply had a hard time giving one another a vote of confidence in our new endeavors. We could no longer generate the same enthusiastic, "Yes, we're with you," that we had always assumed. So at times, one or another of us felt alone or abandoned because we missed the support of the group.

As distance widened among us as a result of our individuation, various aspects of our former life together began to look different. Tending the collective was no longer the priority it used to be. We each managed our own life energy. We began relying more on our individual wisdom and acting autonomously without consulting the group about personal decisions. For some of us who contemplated living by ourselves, money suddenly became an issue. Forms of intimacy were changing. Over time, we quit having nude morning gatherings, although we started having times for massage and other forms of touch. Our sexual relationships were evolving, and some of us were exploring relationships with people outside the family.

Throughout this time, the compassionate techniques we had learned for responsibly communicating about difficult emotions or conflicts helped us navigate these changes. We also realized the importance of forgiving ourselves, one another, and Joe for our failings. Throughout the years that the ten of us were together, many of us, in trying to live up to our ideals, ended up feeling like we had fallen short and judging ourselves. Now we developed a deep respect for ourselves and one another. We also felt a deep respect and appreciation for our friends and colleagues. We became humbler than in the well-oiled machine days, admitting that we didn't have all the answers.

Becoming a Living System

Slowly but surely, we underwent a profound transformation individually and collectively in the four years following Joe's death. During our Us days, we came up with two images that helped us find our place during this process. This was a time of putting everything into the pot, just as the time in Mexico had been. Someone commented, "It's taken two years to break us down to soup, but here we are as soup, and what will we turn into?" So we started using the image of a cauldron where everything gets stirred together, and in the alchemy of the heat and stirring, something new is born. We also imagined us all inside a bulb buried underground where it was dark and we couldn't see any future other than this. Our goal was to cooperate with the unknown.

A year after Joe's death, I wrote in my journal:

We are already creating a new way of being together that is powerful and potent and can bring our highest aspirations to the world. It will likely be different in process and product than if Joe were here, but this is a new game with new rules that we make up (within the framework of the Truths we know to be true).

When I came across *Shaping the Coming Age of Religious Life* by Lawrence Cada, et al., outlining the phases a religious community typically experiences in the course of its life, I was tremendously excited. I recognized where our group was in this cycle, even though we weren't a religious community per se. The phases were foundation, expansion, stabilization, breakdown and conflict, darkness and exploration, and either transformation and revitalization or extinction.

Our group, in one form or another, had gone through the foundation period (Mexico, homesteading in Wisconsin, and building the UV), the expansion period (the UV Family going on the road to be of service and the beginning of NRM), and the stabilization period (NRM's heyday). Now we had just finished the worst of the breakdown and conflict phase and were in the midst of darkness and exploration. We could only hope this would bring individual and group revitalization and transformation. But it could also lead to extinction.

How do you know when you've achieved your mission? And when a group has fulfilled the mission it has gathered for, how does it allow itself to transform? Time would tell how we would fare. But it was heartening to see where we were, that we were not alone, and that the way out was through—i.e., allowing the darkness and exploration period to continue as long as it needed to.

Several years prior, Marilynn had read *The Universe Story: From the Primordial Flaring Forth to the Ecozoic Era—A Celebration of the Unfolding of the Cosmos* by physicist Brian Swimme and geologian Thomas Berry and been profoundly moved by the story they told of how the Universe had come into being and humanity's place in the evolution of the cosmos. We had heard and taken to heart

Sister Miriam MacGillis's talk, "Fate of the Earth," putting Berry's work in the context of our times and asking, "How do we envision an alternative future powerful enough to transform the destructive forces that threaten the fate of the Earth?" Now we watched Swimme's twelve-part video series *Canticle to the Cosmos*, where he described what is known about the story of the Universe from the new physics, including quantum physics, and then how that applied to our very human lives. I, in particular, was inspired by these. For example, Swimme talked about how *allurement* (being drawn toward something) works in the Universe as a positive force and that humans can use their allurements to help discern what they should be doing. For me, this took allurement out of the category of a self-serving drive to something that could give me information about my next steps.

While we were integrating these fresh images and insights and applying them to our group and to ourselves personally, I read *A Simpler Way* by Margaret J. Wheatley and Myron Kellner-Rogers and Wheatley's *Leadership and the New Science: Learning about Organization from an Orderly Universe*. The light bulb went on that we as a group were transforming from a well-oiled machine to a *living system*. We began to see how the well-oiled machine had become stifling and didn't serve us anymore, and how our living system was becoming more dynamic and resilient. It allowed for—even demanded—our individuation and the diversity resulting from that. And we realized it was *family*, not NRM, that was the living system.

The principles that stood out for me from Wheatley's books as most relevant for our group were:

- Responding creatively to what's happening now in an organic and unfolding process rather than being locked into how we've always done it.
- Being clear in our identity but open to how we might change and evolve. Focusing on the aliveness of individuals. If individuals are thriving and following their allurements, then we are moving in the right direction.

- Being prepared for rapid and continuous change. Change must be occurring somewhere in a healthy system all the time.
- Participating more and planning less. Play, creativity, experimentation, and the inherent messiness and redundancy that come from them is not a waste of time but has a greater capacity to solve problems than the well-oiled machine efficiencies.
- Counting on the self-organizing capacity of the Universe to create order instead of being bogged down by the complexities of the organization we created with its structure, policies, and roles.
- Focusing on what will foster the natural emergence of whatever is to come next, such as:
  ◊ Freedom, curiosity, and openness to explore new connections, new information, and new ways of being.
  ◊ Increased flow-through of people and information and being more permeable to the world.
  ◊ Interdependence, everyone being leaderful.
  ◊ Flexibility and going with the flow.

We started calling ourselves the System Sisters. We would have System Circle evenings where we discussed how these principles could help us understand what was happening to us and how to move forward more skillfully. We used the concepts from living systems as affirmation of this disconcerting transformation we were experiencing and as guidelines for how to proceed, breathing fresh air into our lives and process and ways of being.

For a while, I took on leadership of this aspect of our lives. There was irony in this because my skills and training were ideal for creating a well-oiled machine and keeping it humming, and I was probably the one most wedded to the well-oiled machine ways. Change had always been hard for me. But I was suffering like everyone else, and I was on fire with Wheatley's ideas. I saw ways for us to escape the untenable and unhappy place we were stuck in and reinvent ourselves as an organization or cast off our organizational mode and see what new system emerged.

Part of what I brought to the group was the use of mind maps to help us visualize where we had come from, where we were now, and where we might be going. One I called Reinventing Us As a Living System, and another I called The Hand of God. In part, I did these mind maps to help myself understand the bewildering events that had happened so far.

At some point, I became so immersed in my own inner process that I didn't have the energy or focus to lead our group forward. To some, it seemed like I dropped the ball, and I probably did. I often wonder how or if our future would have been different if I had been able to continue providing this leadership.

Meanwhile, Paula was being inspired by Starhawk's *Truth or Dare: Encounters with Power, Authority, and Mystery* and *The Spiral Dance: A Rebirth of the Ancient Religion of the Goddess* and taught us some chants she learned that seemed to capture the spirit of this time period. They evoked the nature of our process—fluid, circular, weaving, being both the changers and the changed. They became our theme songs and provided a lift to our energy when it was flagging.

Our Living System

Despite my stepping away from leadership, our evolution into a living system was unstoppable. Change was a constant, happening rapidly and continuously. "That was then; this is now" became our slogan, even though traditionalists like me still had resistance, at least internally. We had been holding on too tightly to information, control, desired outcomes, and processes. Now we were constantly asking ourselves which ways of doing things were outmoded and which we should hold on to—and why.

We were learning to self-design at the edge of chaos, always asking what would foster our liberation. We trusted that all our new interests were the Universe exploring us in new ways. It became vital to reinfuse ourselves and the group with an energy of forward motion—of "Yes!" We needed to reframe mistakes as accepted aspects of our living system. We were constantly trying to make meaning out of our evolving lives.

On one of our Us days, we asked, "What is needed and wanted for pivotal change to happen in the world?," to find our place in the bigger picture. In the ensuing brainstorming, what emerged was a mandala with four quadrants, which we labeled Reclaiming the Sacred, Treasuring People, Living Fully in a Finite World, and Acting on Behalf of the World. The attitude we wanted to bring to any work in these quadrants was active reverence. This was a wonderful blueprint for what we thought needed to happen in the world. But as time went on, it became apparent that we as a group weren't going to be able to take on any significant portion of it. It was up to each of us as individuals to see where we fit in.

Concepts that described our group at this point were cognitive dissonance, dynamic tension and holding of opposites, dynamic serenity and serene dynamism, active reverence and reverent activism, and loving engagement and engaged loving.

We were reweaving and reinventing, spurred on by the dynamic tensions we were holding:

- The collective versus individual—creating a balance between group coherence and individual freedom, between group synergy and individual action.
- Waiting patiently for vision to emerge versus the attitude of "Now is the time."
- Moving forward on new things versus completing past projects.
- Those of us in slow mode versus those of us in fast mode.

During this time, our inner focus and outer participation happened simultaneously. Many of us wanted more space for a contemplative life while still actively engaged in the world. Each person needed a different balance.

As in the well-oiled machine days, we still wanted our engagement with the world to flow out of Spirit, and our shared spiritual foundation remained intact. But we no longer embraced a shared mission and purpose like in the old days. However, we could agree that we were all part of the Great Work, a term Thomas Berry used in *The Great Work: Our Way into the Future*. He described the Great Work of our time as carrying out "the transition from a period of human devastation of the Earth to a period when humans would be present to the planet in a mutually beneficial manner."

With some of us involved in more inner pursuits while others were more involved in our work in the world or other outer pursuits, our definition of *we* was evolving. We realized that family and team were separate entities.

Vicki describes it this way:

Rather than being a tight team that meets every morning and meets every night and plots and plans and celebrates together, there's a much looser structure where it's more like a family and people come and go. We are constantly celebrating one another's lives but not actively engaged with each other all the time.

When we considered how big our we is, we came up with many answers: the nine of us, our extended family, and the household, which over this time period included some new members.

And we became parts of overlapping circles because of our diversity of new interests and pursuits: Centering Prayer; the mysticism of Joel Goldsmith; Vicki's new, "cool friends;" the Methodist church; praying for both personal healing and healing for the web of life with a community of people who followed Earth traditions; Lakota spirituality; my budding relationship with a man named Birch; nonviolent communication; and the Alternatives to Violence Project, to name a few.

Unraveling and Diaspora

Despite all the changes we were going through, I still thought we would stay together as a family, continuing the work and living the ideals we had said yes to. We were up to something that was greater than Joe, something that would continue whether Joe was there or not. Monica was also sure we would go on. She felt we were strongly bonded and thought she could be far more effective being part of this group than anything she could do on her own.

But without Joe's magnetism providing the centrifugal force that had kept us together, the centripetal forces of this era were too strong, and we began to fly apart. In the four years following Joe's death, six of our group moved out. Diane had moved out within months of his death, finding a home and meaning at the Wilderness Awareness School in Duvall, Washington. Next to leave was Marcia, who eventually moved to Denver to work at Acropolis Books. Here she met the woman who was to become her spiritual teacher in The Infinite Way, a Christian mystical path developed by Joel Goldsmith. Then Lynn moved into a friend's house to begin healing her body and finding herself. She left feeling hurt and confused despite our attempts to understand what was happening for her, and she was determined to look within for guidance. I am grateful and in awe that she has since transcended those feelings even without a satisfactory understanding or resolution.

Soon after Lynn left, Evy enrolled in Union Theological Seminary in New York City to get her Master of Divinity degree to eventually become a Methodist minister. Marilynn had been spending more time exploring Lakota spirituality with Lakota elder Gilbert Walking Bull, who had been mentoring the folks at the Wilderness Awareness School where Diane was now living. She was deeply touched by it, and now she and Diane moved to South Dakota with him to set up a healing center near Pine Ridge, an Oglala Lakota Indian reservation. And finally, Paula moved to a nearby island to do some deep inner work, removing herself from NRM while maintaining her personal connection with our household.

By 2000, there were only three of the ten of us left (Monica, Vicki, and I). Vicki said, "The hand of God is still moving the pieces of this household around." I was really late in saying, "Oh, I guess I need to pick up some aspects of my life too." I wanted our life together and our work to continue, so I just kept taking on more tasks that those who left had been doing. It was becoming unfulfilling and exhausting, but I thought, "I'm going to keep it up because it's important, this is who we are, and we're going to get through this." Eventually, the words erupted out of me, "I can't do it anymore!" I finally recognized that I was no longer thriving and that other parts of me were aching to be born, to be recognized, and to be cultivated.

By 2004, we had all dispersed, one by one, to carry on the vision of love and service in our own ways. As we left the shelter of the group, we each discovered what of our group DNA lived on in us. Vicki said, "Now we have the group DNA thing plus that longtime fidelity to one another's souls. Our job is to continue the work of unconditional love and treasuring people." Marcia said, "It seems to me there are few people I'm in touch with who have experienced something so far from life's usual path, and now we carry a spark of adventure and experience out into our current, unique chosen lives, bringing a contribution, a light, a beacon to our world—and we needn't even speak about it—we *be* it."

This *diaspora* pretty much answered our question about what we women were supposed to be doing or being together—perhaps our work together, at least in the old way, was done. At the time, the diaspora left me with a feeling that we had failed. Neither I nor we could hold the group together without Joe. Over time, as we've gone on to our separate lives, I can see that we each carried the burnished gems of ourselves that were formed in the tumbler of our years together into our new lives. The diaspora led to each of us being out on our own, living our truths in ordinary life. In our own unique ways, we have brought the learnings and experience of our years together into our current lives and work in very beautiful and powerful ways. And we are each more whole and more able to be and express our true selves.

As pollen gathers and disperses, as inlets form and wash away, instances of meaningful community cannot last. Eventually, they will disperse, not because there is something wrong with them, but

because all forms are impermanent and run their cycle. Whether they form for a day or three hundred years, they surface from the reservoir of life-force and eventually join other confluences further downstream. However long, short, wide, or deep a true community might be, its impact is timeless. So the goal is not to make moments of true community last forever, but to inhabit them as fully as possible for as long as possible, and to carry their legacy.[7]

Even though transformation of our group didn't happen, it happened in each individual. For our original group to work as a community and well-oiled machine, we had each needed to be willing to set aside aspects of ourselves and our personal ambitions to be in the UV Family. Meanwhile, the group relationship supported the discovery and development of other facets of our wholeness. And then as we evolved after Joe's death, there was a dissolution of the group relationship and a death and rebirth for each of us. If we came together around the principle of unconditional love and if we stayed aligned with that, the form had to change over time to stay in alignment with love. We set one another free to be the most we could be, as whole beings, fully equipped. We offered one another the opportunity to more fully flower. Vicki said, "Life wants something else from me, and if I confine myself to this structure, I'm not going to give it, and that's hugely painful." For Marcia, the main question was: "How to let the imprisoned splendor escape?" The answer had been community for the years we were together, but now we needed to take the next step—to the individual expression of love.

Vicki said, "We liberated ourselves and one another to find our natural place in the dance of life." Diane's image is that we came from one oak tree, with deep roots and many acorns. Over the years since our diaspora, each of us has grown from our individual acorn that carried the group DNA into our own unique tree, offering something important in the world.

---

[7]Nepo, Mark. *More Together Than Alone: Discovering the Power and Spirit of Community in Our Lives and In the World* (New York, N.Y.: Atria Books, 2018), 3.

I have come to see that there is as much value in what we did after the diaspora as during our years together. Also, I have come to see that the experiment didn't fail. We weren't failures. We could go only so far. Perhaps if the sacrifices hadn't been so great or the shadow so large, we could have embraced that other future. If we took our learnings now and could redo the experiment, perhaps we could go further next time. But not this time. Just as with the story of the Universe, our era of living in community was a one-time event for us, and we can't go back.

Shifts in Our Work

Joe's death marked the onset of a transformation not only of our group but also of our work and NRM. In the months after his death, it was all we could do to keep NRM functioning smoothly and projects moving forward while so much was happening for us in other realms, individually and collectively. Fortunately, our longtime volunteers and others who noticed we were struggling stepped in. They pointed out that they had expertise and experience in running offices, and if we would just let them, they would be happy to help run ours. We have deep gratitude for how they pitched in and helped keep things going.

As each person moved out, those of us left had more responsibilities to shoulder for running NRM, and we could no longer count on our synergy to pull us through. To lighten up about our plight, we took to calling ourselves the Hernia Sisters and the Sisters of Perpetual Responsibility. By the time there were just three of us left, Monica and I were ready to put NRM to bed. But Vicki still had big visions for bringing the FI work to schools, churches, and other institutions, so we kept NRM going. We ended up hiring someone for the first time in our history—an administrative assistant to help us navigate this new territory and help Vicki move forward without her old team.

During this time, Financial Integrity Associates (FIA) was born, a self-empowered, self-organizing network of FIers who had been waiting to be empowered by us to help spread the word about the nine-step program and share their experience and expertise.

Even as the well-oiled machine was disintegrating and the living system was emerging, we still produced a lot for the world. I was only involved tangentially. These accomplishments are due to the hard work of others from our group, especially Vicki and Monica, as well as from our colleagues, especially FIA, this new network of FIers.

Vicki updated *Your Money or Your Life* for the second edition. By then, the book had been translated into eight languages. She also did countless interviews. Monica and several FIA colleagues wrote a Speaker's Bureau manual for the enthusiastic FIA network. Two more study guides, each targeting a different audience, were written to be used with *Your Money or Your Life* by groups or individuals. Online study groups became popular, and the first NRM website was created. Sounds True (a multimedia publishing company offering transformational programs for living a more meaningful life) began producing and selling the old tape course, *Transforming Your Relationship with Money and Achieving Financial Independence*, making it available to a wider audience.

Eventually, with perhaps equal parts of wistfulness, apprehension, and relief, we turned NRM over to someone else to run, with Monica and Vicki remaining on the board for a few years.

Part IV

Reflections and Aftermath

Chapter 14

Who Were We? What Drove Us?

Our community was thirty-five years old when we parted ways in 2004. The four founders came together initially as spiritual seekers—not to create community but to spiritually wake up together. They were influenced and molded by the unfolding times they were living through—the counterculture of the 1960s and 1970s. It was a time of social experimentation, consciousness expansion, and political upheaval.

Upon reflection, it's clear that their spiritual search back then was made easier by their white privilege. Certainly, Joe, as a Latino growing up in Spanish Harlem, did not come from privilege. But the privileged circumstances in which the original four UV Family found themselves in the Mexican fishing village enabled them to devote themselves to uncovering the truths that were relevant to them at the time. And from then on, our group explorations, supportive physical environment, and our work in the world were made easier because of our privilege.

Although our group had coalesced around the spiritual search, natural by-products became family and, eventually, community. The component of service fell into place early on. The change-the-world layer evolved as the times changed.

Around the time I came along in 1984, we took to heart Peter Russell's exhortation in his 1983 film, *The Global Brain*, that "affairs are now soul size. / The enterprise is exploration into God . . . will you wake for pity's sake!" from Christopher Fry's poem in the play *A Sleep of Prisoners*. It became a touchstone for us.

There are different ways to look at who we were and what our years together were about, and in some sense, they are all true.

- It was about learning to love, about being a generator of love. We were a family first, an intentional community second. We took on an experiment—to live in a committed, loving, surrendered relationship with one another and do the work we thought the world was asking of us. We tried to live the unconditional love we had experienced in our relationship with one another. Our community, our work, and our teachings were outgrowths of our relationship and the desire to live our ideals.
- It was about embodying and living on a daily basis the universal life truths as we knew and experienced them.
- It was about cocreation, what we created together. We saw ourselves as a finely honed team to create synergy.
- It was about touching people's lives and serving.
- It was about trying to save the world.

Back in the early 1980s, a good friend and futurist asked the four UV Family members that I had met at Dinosaur National Monument, "Is your relationship just a product of four unique and well-matched people, or is it pro-evolution, a workable model for others and a harbinger of things to come?" They answered "No" to the first question and "Could be" to the second.[8]

I think the same question could be posed to the ten of us who lived and worked together in the NRM house in Seattle, and I would answer the same way. We were ordinary people living something that few people get a chance to experience. We were nine women and one man, living and working together in a stable relationship for ten years

---

[8]The UV Family, "The Possible Relationship: Basic Principles from an Innovative Relationship," *In Context*, summer 1985, https://www.context.org/iclib/ic10/uvfamily/.

(1986–1996). We each called on the highest parts of ourselves, living with love and Spirit as our guides on a daily basis.

Perhaps we created a template that others can step into. I don't imagine or want people to follow our model at the form level, but other groups can make use of this template evoking the essence of our group and express it in their own unique forms.

Chapter 15

Outcome

So what was the outcome? We did our best to embody love, touch people's lives, live our ideals, cocreate together, and serve the world. Our tangible accomplishments included getting *Your Money or Your Life* into the hands of a lot of people, helping to embed the frugality movement in North America, getting mind-body research published in a peer-reviewed medical journal, and giving away a million dollars —all while living in an intentional, loving, and committed relationship.

Marcia comments:

We really did do our best, and look what came from this little ragtag group! We found a way beyond our humanness to weave a most meaningful life together, and that beyond big and little obstacles, we accomplished the unthinkable. We really were an example of that little group that Margaret Mead talks about when she says, "Never doubt that a small group of thoughtful, committed citizens can change the world: indeed, it's the only thing that ever has." We were an example of what can happen when a group of people puts their whole heart and soul into something without wanting anything in return ... It took a lot to live that life in terms of what we demanded of ourselves; we stretched ourselves as much as we could.

There was a purity to our vision despite our imperfections in living it. We each said yes to the vision, and it took all of us living as our highest selves to manifest the vision. We each brought our gifts, aptitudes, annoying habits, baggage, dysfunctions, and uniqueness to this group endeavor. Our imperfections were overshadowed by our commitment to love, to our ideal, to inner growth, to honesty, to openness, and to challenging our individual dysfunctions. We each stretched ourselves far beyond what we could have imagined. To the degree that we lived up to our commitments, we functioned harmoniously, individually and as a group. When we lost sight of our commitments, disharmony and dysfunction took over.

Vicki reflects on our idealistic community:

> We carried that precious hope in the human heart that we, as a species, can be better . . . We are all part of a long, human experiment and standing on the shoulders of ones who came before. A strong leader is inherent in idealistic groups—it just has that particular shadow. We were all so well intentioned, so earnest, so dedicated and willing to sacrifice the small for the large . . . It makes me smile with tenderness for that younger set of selves. It so reflects that world we tried to declare into being and that we each lived with so much devotion and so little attention to what our human selves, so lovely and lively, actually needed.

For me, it was a privilege to live with this group of people and to experience the qualities of our heartbeat. I am grateful for all our years together, no matter how hard they were at times. I feel honored to have been part of what felt to me like a sacred undertaking and for the opportunity to make this transformational journey.

> While few practical utopias last for long, utopian living is extraordinarily generative. It creates openings in the fabric of society, inspires change, reminds us that it is possible to reach beyond the dominant assumptions of our day and discover radically different ways of being.[9]

---

[9]Neima, Anna. *The Utopians: Six Attempts to Build the Perfect Society* (London, England: Picador, 2021), 236.

Chapter 16

Where Are We Now?

R eflecting on our experience together, Vicki muses:

Perhaps it's like a mountain we all climbed. The mountain was real. The blood, sweat, and tears were real. We were even roped together. But for each it meant something different in the context of our own destiny. Now we have come down from the mountain and are each traveling our own paths. We are no longer roped together . . . Now we have gone from our extraordinary selves to our ordinary selves.

We have each gone out into the world empowered, following our individual destinies, singing our own heart song. But, at least for me, whenever we are together, our songs become brighter and stronger, creating a harmony that still echoes the symphony we created in our years in community. Whenever some of us from these NRM days get together, we laugh and laugh—at our earnestness, in our delight at being together and feeling the comfort of being so totally known and loved, at our foibles and the fun and stupid things we did.

We still loved and cared about one another enough to gather several times in the years since we disbanded. In some ways, regardless of the intervening years, many of us have the experience that our Sisters know us better than anyone else ever has and probably ever will. A man who met us for the first time at one gathering said that he'd never seen women so harmonious and caring and close, except in twins. That being said, there would still be some wounds from our past that would emerge at each gathering to be received with as much openness, love, and forgiveness as we could muster. Our reunion twenty years after Joe died was poignant because, given our ages, we knew it *could* be the last time all nine of us would be together. And it was.

Each one of us has carried the heartbeat out into the world as we live our separate lives. We are each ministering, but in very different ways. So the heartbeat continues, just in nine different ways.

During and after treatment for colon cancer in 2004, Vicki experienced a period of deep soul-searching and emerged from that time period having shed the drive to save the world. But she is still involved in social and cultural change. She is still engaged in the financial work, and, in the 2018 edition of *Your Money or Your Life*, has adapted our nine-step program for the times we are currently in and for the younger generation. She has published another book, *Blessing the Hands That Feed Us: Lessons from a 10-Mile Diet*, about local relational eating, and is involved in local activism. She continues to be a visionary, a natural leader, an eloquent writer, and a public speaker. She now hosts a podcast, *What Could Possibly Go Right?*

Monica has continued to offer the people she meets an experience of unconditional love and acceptance, whether in her work in prisons with the Alternatives to Violence Project, her weekly Centering Prayer meditation group, leading Centering Prayer retreats and otherwise volunteering with the Contemplative Outreach Northwest community, and in the senior living community where she lives.

Evy loved preaching and being a United Methodist minister for much of the past twenty years. She recently retired from being an assistant pastor at a church in Tucson and is actively listening to God for what her life will entail beyond retirement. No matter what she does, she will remain passionate about promoting diversity and social justice. She is the author of the book *Living as a Covenant Community*, written for United Methodist Women, and will now have the time to finish her book about her personal story of illness and healing.

Diane has grieved the deaths of several partners over the years since leaving NRM. She now lives a quiet life in South Dakota with her new husband. She has a leadership role in an online circle of native and non-native women who meet weekly. She was also guest of honor at the Wilderness Awareness School when they celebrated the twentieth anniversary of the late Gilbert Walking Bull's role in mentoring their community. Attending an Agape Spiritual Center and offering loving attention to others in need are important focuses of her life.

Marilynn's life is an expression of her dedication to the Lakota spiritual path. She resides at Tatanka Mani Camp (the Lakota term that means "Buffalo Walking"), the healing center that Gilbert, she, and Diane cofounded near Hot Springs, South Dakota. Through her caring, she has developed strong friendships with many people on the Pine Ridge Indian Reservation. For many years, she has hosted, along with friends from the reservation, a Motivated to Live leadership camp each summer for youth from Pine Ridge. For the past fifteen years, she worked with a team of women providing food, warm clothing, and gifts at Christmastime for up to fifteen families and one hundred children on the reservation.

Paula lives with her partner in Massachusetts and has served as a volunteer Network Weaver for the international Work That Reconnects Network. She continues to respond, as best she can, to the foundational NRM query: "How can my life be of service?"

Lynn is a classical pianist and teacher, sharing her spirit and soul through music. Encountering and recovering from illness (environmentally induced and cancer) has been part of her spiritual journey for many years. Her spiritual practice is based on a set of esoteric teachings in what is called a *mystery school*. Like siblings, she says, we all had very different experiences. But what she remembers now is the love.

Marcia was part of a spiritual group led by her teacher in The Infinite Way. She transcribed a number of her teacher's talks and edited many of the booklets that were produced on these teachings. She also led a "calling tree" prayer circle for The Infinite Way. Marcia said of her years with us, "I have a deep appreciation for what was given to me during my participation in the [Grand] Adventure and how I've built my life on all that was positive...I'm out in the world in this adventuresome spirit." For her, it was so important to live her highest, *in freedom*, with emphasis on that feeling of internal freedom. "I'm out in the world in peace."

In early 2018, Marcia was diagnosed with glioblastoma, an aggressive brain cancer, and died four months later. Soon after her diagnosis, she began feeling a great sense of freedom and peace. And right before surgery, she said, "It's totally okay for me to die, and I've had an incredible life." Monica and I were able to spend ten days with her after her surgery while she was still able to talk and be somewhat active. While we were there, all nine of us women circled up via Zoom to do a recognition ceremony for Marcia. This allowed us all to tell her what she meant to us, recount stories from our years together, and say goodbye. She told us she loved us and that she was at peace with dying.

The rest of our in-person visit with Marcia was spent reminiscing, laughing, and showing our love in as many ways as we could. We listened to *Graceful Passages: A Companion for Living and Dying*, a book and CD set produced by Michael Stillwater and Gary Malkin that contains reflections on the process of dying and death by various spiritual teachers. Monica pointed out that the rhythmic ker-thump of Marcia's oxygen concentrator felt like us being held in the heartbeat of the world. The three of us had one last, precious Heart Sharing. And Monica and I sang "Long Time Sun" by Snatam Kaur to Marcia as our final blessing when we left. When she died, there was nothing left unsaid or undone, and no regrets. Just love and gratitude. Marcia taught us so much about dying and death just by her example.

I miss Marcia in so many ways. I found I relied on her for her counsel and her acceptance of me. She was also a champion of this book project, and over the years, we had many conversations to try to understand various aspects of our lives together. I valued her insights. As I revise the ending of this book to include her death, my heartache is acute.

And where is Joe now? A whiff of black Cavendish pipe tobacco tickles my nose as I open an envelope of letters and memorabilia from my early days with the UV Family. There's Joe! Hi, Joe! You're still here, twenty-five years after you died. A whole thread of life with Joe evoked in that whiff. Those papers have been tucked away for probably thirty years, carefully preserving not just love letters from all four of the UV Family I met at Dinosaur National Monument, but also the essence of Joe. There he is, tap, tap, tapping his pipe; giving his little smoker's cough; clicking the lighter; and allowing the smoke to take him to new thoughts, outlandish ideas, and sometimes getting to the crux of a matter. I didn't like the smoke, but it was part of the package I bought when I joined the family. And now it serves as a sweet reminder of Joe.

Chapter 17

Where Am I?

As One Doorway Begins to Close, Another Opens

Just as my Grand Adventure with NRM began when I first met Evy hiking down the trail in Dinosaur National Monument, so too does my next big adventure begin when I am hiking on a trail the year before Joe died. This time it is at Hart's Pass in the North Cascades of Washington State. Coming toward me is a man with an unkempt beard, wearing a well-worn brimmed hat and leading a string of pack donkeys. I step off the trail onto the steep rocky slope to let them pass. He can't stop to say more than hi, but something about his being leaves a lasting impression on me, and I want to know more about him.

A year later, I am in deep grief about Joe's death eight months before and have a profound need to be in the wilderness, where I can grieve, feel nourished, and find my wholeness. I have hauled my gear into an unofficial campsite a mile from the parking lot at Hart's Pass and have just set up camp. I'm glad to have ten days to be totally alone to process this grief and the emptiness I feel. But now I hear the tinkle of bells, and along comes this same man, leading his string of donkeys.

Despite my curiosity about this man named Birch, I am distraught that my aloneness has been interrupted. It turns out that he has been camping below me in between his pack trips and intends to camp there tonight. I am on my way to haul more water from the parking lot to my site, and he offers a donkey to carry my water. I am struck by his immediate trust in me, but I have never been around a large animal, so I decline. I sob on the way to my car, still distraught, but then realize I need to at least be civil and ask him to my campsite for tea.

I don't know it yet, but another doorway has opened in my life, and I'm about to walk through it.

My Current Life

Birch and I found we shared a deep spiritual foundation, and our interactions at Hart's Pass touched my heart and deep longing to be cherished by a man once again. After a couple of years of soul-searching on my part, we started a relationship. He lived in Winthrop in the Methow Valley in the foothills of the North Cascades in eastern Washington. For five years, I traveled back and forth between Seattle and Winthrop as I helped wind up our lives at NRM and tried to reach clarity about my next step. In 2004, I left NRM and moved to Winthrop.

Now I live a quiet, rural life in a beautiful, natural setting of sagebrush hills and ponderosa pine forests with Birch and just a couple of donkeys now that he is retired. I spend time in nature as often as possible. It was a huge adjustment from living in community to living with one other person. I needed Birch's gentle presence, the quiet, and the access to nature, but I missed the dynamism and laughter of my NRM family—and still do. But I have no regrets about ending that part of my life because it had ended for all of us long before I left. It took me all that time to finally let go and accept that it was over.

Owning my experience and inner truth has been a many-year process, requiring me to pick up the thread of individuation I left when I surrendered my individual life to the needs of the whole at NRM. I had to ask, "Who am I now?," and do that work of individuation. I finally know who I am now, am more at peace with myself, more fully rounded, more creative, skilled at emotional inquiry of myself and others, and have a greater capacity for depth. I am grateful beyond measure for our years together and am still connected with all the Sisters.

As I tried to find my own heart song, I often asked myself what I had learned and embodied from my years with the UV Family. After all, I don't exemplify some of the hallmark features of the family: early adoption of new ideas, curiosity, chutzpah. My style is reserved and introverted. I really don't live in the spirit of a Grand Adventure anymore. I typically don't say yes to God-size tasks or go beyond known limits. I'm not a leading-edge thinker or activist.

So if I'm not that, what did I carry forward? Well, I do still carry the group DNA. Looking back, I can see just how much this group of people and our work helped me transform my life. I am still committed to spiritual growth, deep reflection, and a spiritual practice. I have tools to use when dealing with troublesome thoughts, emotions, attitudes, and behaviors. I have cultivated a trust in the divine unfolding of my life and have more resilience and acceptance when things don't go my way.

Love of myself and others is foundational to my sense of self. I seek depth and intimacy in all my relationships, and I can see and reflect back the magnificence of another person. I listen deeply and try to treat others with respect and kindness. I love providing a supportive space to hold and accompany others on their soul journeys.

I aspire to support and champion younger people who are passionate about doing their part to make the world a better place. As major, unexpected national or world events provide openings for something new to happen, I want to be there encouraging and assisting young people who are ready to walk through those open doors. I mentor a youngish woman who has a vision of how she wants to love and serve, and she appreciates my caring and guidance as a gentle elder.

I still create and nurture community. In my inner life, I explore the depths of myself and then share my learnings with the groups I belong to. I help create a safe container (an emotionally safe space) and look out for the well-being of the whole group. I can step into a leadership position when needed. My intention is to create an environment where our hearts and souls can speak and we feel heard. I am a voice for compassion for myself and others. Sometimes I experience the synergy I miss so much—of sharing ideas and inspirations and building off one another or working on projects together.

I lead a group in SoulCollage®, a process of using collage to access parts of one's soul, developed by Seena Frost in *SoulCollage® Evolving:*

An Intuitive Collage Process for Self-Discovery & Community. Making and sharing collages in a group often brings out "magic" and unexpected insights. I was active in a spiritual study group for many years, as well as a healing circle where we used healing touch to bring healing energy to ourselves, others, and the world. Now I help lead a group of six women exploring a different theme each year. One year, we studied Stephen Levine's *A Year to Live: How to Live This Year As If It Were Your Last* and asked ourselves how we could live more fully. Another year, we asked, "What is mine to do at this phase of my life and given the times we live in?" During another, we undertook a yearlong rite of passage into elderhood.

At the age of sixty-three, I spent a month camping alone in the Anza-Borrego Desert in California at our old site. This was a dream come true for me—part personal and spiritual renewal, part immersion in nature, and part completion of my years with the UV Family. In the vastness, subtle beauty, and quiet of that desert, I expanded and let my inner wisdom reveal itself.

I do miss the excitement and fulfillment of a grand purpose and the ongoing synergy we experienced. I miss the symphony, and I miss being seen so deeply. And I miss the laughter.

As I reflect on what is most different in me from my days in community, it is an acceptance and embrace of my own humanity. This has allowed me to be kinder to myself, less self-righteous and judgmental of others, and able to embrace others in their humanness. I still have my idealism, but it is tempered by a sense of our shared humanity.

Conclusion

This group of people has journeyed deeply together, and our bond remains strong. Some of us are wistful about various aspects of our life together in community but realize we aren't going to re-create this in our individual lives now. Our job is to continue the work of unconditional love, treasuring people, and responding to calls from Lola.

Vicki says, "Our creation of our worldview and community and work was our great gift to others. It was collective art, a collective donation to the great chain of being, the temple we built to God. We have given up being artists of that collective work, yet we are each curators."

For the past twenty years, writing this book has been an expression of my role as a curator of our collective work. I have felt a consistent and deep inner desire to evoke for you this heartbeat we all lived and to show the facets of the diamond we created. Now, when you hold this diamond in your hand, what shines brightest for you in your own life?

The current times want something different than the times our group lived through, but the inspiration to do something to make a difference is the same. The ten-year window of opportunity in the 1990s that Noel Brown said we had to reverse global warming has come and gone. Consumption of fossil fuels has continued to rise, the Arctic and Antarctic ice caps are melting, sea levels are rising, and weather has become more extreme. And climate disruption is but one of the many worsening crises of our time.

Living in community, working together in groups, and building caring relationships wherever we are is part of what's being called for to address these issues. Sharing resources and living low-consumption, high-fulfillment lifestyles are even more important today than in the era of our group.

For younger people, I hope this book provides some insight that can help illuminate your way to a new world even as the old world crumbles. It is your turn to call forth your passion and bring into existence what is being evoked by these times. It is a time for you travel to the edges of your own frontier, coming back stronger, wiser, and more whole in yourself. I hope to be your champion, supporting your endeavors and lauding your courage. I offer you respect, blessings, encouragement, and strength for the journey.

A group with a heartbeat is a precious thing. My hope is that you already have one or more groups with a strong heartbeat in your life. If you live in community now or have lived in one in the past, perhaps you experience this heartbeat daily or carry a piece of it with you as you move through your life. If not, maybe you will be inspired to take on the challenge and adventure of community—not to mimic our form, which was certainly imperfect, but to take on collectively something that brings forth your passion and let it evolve.

May all of us, wherever we are on life's journey, follow where the heartbeat leads us.

Acknowledgments

The many conversations I have had with my NRM Sisters reflecting on our years together have been integral to this writing. All of them had the opportunity to read this book and voice any major concerns. They offered valuable perspectives, corrections, and additions, most of which made their way into the book. I deeply appreciate their graciousness in respecting my impulse to tell this story.

Heartfelt gratitude to Marge Osborn, who was the midwife for this book. She was my writing mentor and cheerleader. She read my first drafts and gave substantive but kind suggestions and comments. When I got discouraged, she reminded me that this story deserved to be written and read. I am not at all sure I would be holding this book in my hand without her guidance and support.

Monica Wood, Paula Hendrick, and Carol Harley read various drafts and provided thoughtful feedback on content as well as doing extensive editing. Monica shepherded me through many deliberations regarding word usage and difficult subjects, as well as checking for accuracy.

Thank you to others who read previous drafts and offered useful suggestions: Darcy Ottey, Marisa Withey-Byrne, Nancy Farr, Susan Speir, and Betsy Weiss. And special gratitude to my women's circle for being my champions and offering encouragement and wise counsel when I most needed it. Thanks to my partner, Birch Berman, for his respect and support for the years I disappeared into my studio to write this book over the last two decades. He trusted in me without knowing exactly what I was up to until he finally read a recent draft. ("Now I know what you've been doing in the studio all these years!") His critical feedback and ideas helped me find better ways to express what I wanted to say.

I'm grateful to my sister Peggy Norris for helping me navigate the steps to self-publishing. A big thank you to my niece Libby Norris for her artistic sensibilities and experience and her patience in working with me to design the book cover. Many thanks to the folks at Kirkus Review doing the copyediting and layout.

A few friends and extended family were especially important in my years with the UV Family. As I have already mentioned, Alan Seid, Tricia King, and Margaret "Tree" Moore were important companions on the journey. Phil Notermann and Helen Gabel, who entered our lives when they were doing the nine-step program, joined our household a few years after Joe died, having reached financial independence by that time. They had been living in community for many years and brought with them a much needed infusion of fresh energy, optimism, and their innate compassion and wisdom.

Sue Wiedenfeld and Al Hillel, in addition to being essential collaborators on the ALS Project, brought their curiosity about the spiritual life and their caring to our whole group. Jacquelyn Blix and the late David Heitmiller were avid FIers who became both colleagues and friends of ours. They went on to write their own book, *Getting a Life: Real Lives Transformed by Your Money or Your Life,* about their experience of doing the nine-step program and becoming financially independent. Jason Weston caught the spirit of our group when he was in his twenties, and he and Joe would have long talks together in the UV. When Vicki and Monica were ready to let go of the UV, they gave it to Jason. He refurbished it and still uses it, more than forty-five years after it was built.

I want to acknowledge our wider circle of extended family and friends who traveled alongside us over the years, being companions on the journey; the myriad volunteers who were willing and dedicated supporters of us and our work; and other groups, colleagues, and collaborators who crossed our path and inspired us by their work of bringing more compassion and sustainability to the world. Special thanks to Helen and Kees Kolff and the late Joyce Doan for their dear friendship and collaborations through Beyond War. Dawn Raymond inspired me with her vibrancy, competency, and sincere quest for transformation and Jim Merkel by his earnestness and daily demonstration of living his values of simplicity and living lightly on the earth. Gurudhan Khalsa, volunteer extraordinaire, touched my heart deeply.

Special gratitude to Sister Miriam MacGillis for the inspiration of her work at Genesis Farm and with earth literacy, for her appreciation of Joe, and for the support and wise perspectives she offered me and our group after he died. She was a mentor to me when I most needed it as I was grieving Joe's death and struggling with the changes in our group. Thank you to Sarah Knoebber for being supportive of my book idea early on and offering questions and suggestions about what she'd like to see in the book.

Much appreciation to Hypatia-in-the-Woods in Shelton, Washington, for providing a two-week writing residency, where I was able to finish my first full draft.

I want to recognize the indigenous peoples of the lands I lived on, visited, and loved. I grew up in the territory of the Erie and Mississauga tribes. Juneau, Alaska, is on the land of the Tlingit people. Dinosaur National Monument resides on the ancestral land of the prehistoric Fremont peoples and, more recently, the Ute and Shoshone tribes. Fort Collins is on the land of the Arapaho, Cheyenne, and Ute nations. Jenner is on the lands of the Kashaya and Graton Rancheria peoples. Seattle is home to the Duwamish tribe. Anza-Borrego Desert State Park is on the ancestral lands of the Kumeyaay and Cahuilla peoples. Winthrop is home to the Methow tribe.